P9-CQG-173

WWF
WAR
ZONE™

By

Jacob McBane

BradyGAMES
STRATEGY GUIDES

Table of Contents

Totally Unauthorized WWF™ War Zone™ Pocket Guide

©1998 All rights reserved, including the right of reproduction in whole or in part in any form.

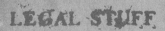

LEGAL STUFF

Brady Publishing

An Imprint of

Macmillan Digital Publishing USA

201 W. 103rd St., Indianapolis, IN 46290

ISBN: 1-56686-815-7

Library of Congress Catalog No.: 98-073165

BradyGAMES STAFF

Publisher
Lynn Zingraf

Editor-In-Chief
H. Leigh Davis

Title/Licensing Manager
David Waybright

Marketing Manager
Janet Cadoff

Acquisitions Editor
Debra McBride

CREDITS

Development Editor
David Cassady

Project Editor
Tim Cox

Screenshot Editor
Michael Owen

Creative Director
Scott Watanabe

Book Designer
Max Adamson

Production Designer
Dan Caparo

Chapter 1

Welcome to the Ring, Baby

You thought you were tough, you thought you were bad, but then you stepped into the ring and were taught the meaning of pain—real pain. Steve Austin left you "stone cold" and The Undertaker quickly sent you to the not-so-sweet hereafter—and that was just during the warm-ups! While you are indeed being taught a lesson, it's not exactly the kind of wrestling instruction you want or need.

That's where this handy-dandy pocket guide comes in to play. Between the covers lies everything you need to know to reach the top and become king of the ring.

In this chapter, we'll discuss the basic controls of the game, whether your platform of choice is the Sony PlayStation or the Nintendo 64.

In Chapter 2, we'll cover the game basics. In particular, we'll analyze all the important and damaging moves that can be found in the War Zone that is the WWF. We'll also touch on the different modes of play, such as "Challenge" and "Tag Team," giving you the stuff you need to succeed.

Chapter 3 introduces you to the enemy (or your wrestler of choice, depending on how you look at things). We'll show you all the moves for all the wrestlers, discuss his strengths and weaknesses, and what to expect from each wrestler—whether he's in your corner or the enemy. We'll also list each wrestler's **Secret Moves**, the ones that you won't learn from any Training Mode—the stuff that you'll use to wipe up the competition.

To make things easier for the reader, we made sure you could easily find each wrestler's **SECRET MOVES**. All the **SECRET MOVES** appear in red, so you can quickly pick them out from the regular moves.

Well, what are you waiting for? Jump in the ring and prepare to battle the fight of your life!

Game Controls

Whether you're using a PS or an N64, it pays to know your buttons.

PlayStation

D-Pad:	Moves the wrestler left, right, up, and down.
Triangle:	Punch/Throw weapon
Circle:	Tieup/Pin/Pick up weapon
X:	Block
Square:	Kick
L1:	Dodge left
L2:	Dodge right
R1:	Toggle between opponents/climb Turnbuckle and back into the ring
R2:	Run

Nintendo 64

D-Pad/Joystick:	Moves the wrestler left, right, up, and down.
B:	Punch/Throw weapon
A:	Kick
C-Up:	Toggle between opponents/climb Turnbuckle and back into the ring
C-Right:	Run
C-Down:	Block
C-Left:	Tieup/Pin/Pick up weapon
L Shift:	Dodge left
R Shift:	Dodge right

Chapter 1

Chapter 2

Master the Basics: The Basics of Wrestling

You wouldn't even consider climbing behind the wheel of a car if you didn't know the difference between a steering wheel and a brake pedal, now would ya? So why would you climb into the ring without knowing a suplex from a DDT? In this chapter, we're going to get you up to speed on all you need to know about the important moves found in **WWF War Zone**.

Keep one thing in mind: Although some buttons do the same thing for all the wrestlers (like Punch and Kick), different wrestlers have different key combinations for the same move. So while pressing Up, Down, Tieup will make Steve Austin perform an Overhead Belly Belly Suplex, that same key combination will make Thrasher execute the Samoan Drop. The key is to pick which wrestler is your favorite and learn the key combos for his moves.

On the next several pages, we'll take a look at many of the moves featured in **WWF War Zone**. We'll cover the ones you'll want to be most familiar with, either because of their easy execution, or because of their high damage points (or maybe even both). Master these moves (along with the secret ones mentioned in Chapter 3) and you'll become a wrestling machine!

The Moves, the Mayhem

The Punch

The most basic of moves, the punch is just the thing to momentarily daze your opponent long enough to set him up for the killer move you've been hiding up your sleeve (if you were wearing any). It doesn't pack much damage, but better him than you!

The Quick Kick

A Quick Kick to the gut works wonders for your gameplan. Although like its low damage brother, the Punch, it doesn't cause too much hurtin', however, you can quickly lower your opponent's health with a few quick boots to the belly, setting yourself up to perform a more serious maneuver.

The Tieup

Just in case you've been spending your days in a cave, almost all of your really deadly moves will end up being performed by using the Tieup. If you find that your opponent has wisened up to your incessant punching and kicking, it's a good idea to quickly move into a Tieup to quickly dish out some serious pain.

The Whip

This basic move will quickly have your character grabbing his opponent and whipping him into one of two places. He'll get launched either A). into the turnbuckle, which feels none too good (plus you can race over and whomp on him some more) or B). into the ropes, where he'll come helplessly flying back to either a clothesline with the Punch or a Quick Kick.

The Arm Drag

This quick and dirty move allows for the easy flipping of an opponent. Although it doesn't exactly rack up the damage points, you'll no doubt impress your friends with it (especially if they're the victims).

'The Arm Wrench

Having your elbow pulled back behind your ears isn't anyone's idea of a good time. Although it doesn't inflict a whole lot of damage, this great follow-up to the Arm Drag is fun to watch as your opponent squirms in pain.

'The Bearhug

This move is exactly what the name implies. Even though it may not look terribly impressive, it dishes out plenty of hurt, as well as sending a few opponents to the chiropractor's office.

'The Bodyslam

When you think of wrestling (WWF wrestling, anyway) this is what you think of—Bodyslams that send the opponent flat on his back on the mat. This is as devastating as a Bearhug, if not more so (depending on the wrestler) but looks a whole lot cooler.

'The Crucifix

For all the athleticism this move seemingly requires, it sure doesn't cause much in the way of damage. With this move, you wrap around your opponent, sending him backwards to the floor, thereby dishing out some hurt for a few seconds. It looks cool, but is better left for those merely trying to impress, rather than win.

'Fireman's Carry

Make no mistake, you aren't trying to carry anyone to safety, but merely trying to inflict as much bodily harm in as short a time as possible. Although this isn't what you would call a damage maker, it's usually relatively easy to quickly execute, making it ideal in most Ready situations.

'The Hiptoss

The Hiptoss is another quick and painful move that will send the opponent to the mat. Like the Fireman's Carry, this move looks more harmful than it really is, but it too is relatively easy to pull off and stuns your opponent enough to execute a deadlier move.

'DDT

There's nothin' like poundin' your opponent's head into the mat to send chills up both your spines. Use the DDT as a follow-up to a Quick Kick or Punch for maximum impact.

'Gut Wrench

Now we're getting into some serious pain when you're talking about a Gut Wrench. It's usually easy to execute and carries a world of hurt as well, so use it whenever your opponent has paused to catch his breath.

'The Japanese Arm Drag

This is another cool-looking move that looks better than it actually is. The Japanese Arm Drag usually only causes 2 or 3 points of damage, so you might as well opt for the Gut Wrench or even the DDT before resorting to this move.

'Kneebreaker

Bringing your opponent to his knees is just what you were hoping for, and this little number does just the trick. Although it looks like your opponent has you around the neck, don't worry–he's the one holding on for dear life!

'Neckbreaker

In case the Kneebreaker just isn't punishment enough, there's the Neckbreaker, which helps put the kinks back in your opponent's neck where they belong. This move almost always causes more damage than the Kneebreaker, so don't be afraid to use it when the opportunity presents itself.

'Samoan Drop

This devastating move is found in almost every wrestler's inventory of killer moves. When executing the Samoan Drop, you pick up the opponent like in the Fireman's Carry, but you stand up all the way and then fall backwards, using your foe to cushion your blow. Although it's tough to execute, those with nimble fingers will have no problem if they're quick, especially if they've managed to temporarily rattle their opponent to set up for it.

'Single Arm DDT

How about sending your opponent straight to the mat face first with no way to cushion his own blow? If that's your idea of a good time, then you'll love this baby because that's exactly what this move does. The Single Arm DDT causes just as much damage as the Samoan Drop.

'Side Belly Belly Suplex

This little move is sure to inflict plenty o' damage no matter which wrestler executes it. By picking up your opponent and going belly to belly with him before slamming him to the mat, you're sure to inflict at least 6 points of damage before he even knows what hit him. Use this move as often as possible, especially when you've just stunned him with a Quick Kick.

'The Spinebuster

The Spinebuster not only looks cool, but it's accompanied by the loud sound of bones snapping. This major damage maker is just what the doctor didn't order. You pick up your opponent, and then drive him butt first into the mat, theoretically collapsing his spine at the same time.

'Power Bomb

Speaking of serious damage, moves don't get much more painful than the Power Bomb, which has been known to register a 9 on the hurtin' scale. With this move, you lift up your opponent nearly over your head, and drive his back straight into the mat. The Power Bomb is perfect whenever you find yourself in a Tieup, and it will make your opponent think twice before fighting you again.

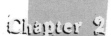

Chapter 2

'Double Underhook Suplex

This baby, in most cases, causes at least an 8 on the damage meter, and boy does it show! You reach over the top of your opponent, grab his arms, and then flip him end over end straight into the mat. This is another excellent Tieup maneuver that's sure to be a crowd pleaser.

'Top Rope Superplex

This is arguably the coolest move in the game. Having stunned your opponent into the turnbuckle, you then push him up on top, grab him, and flip him over onto his back. Now this is what you call fun!

'Victory Roll

With your opponent dazed and confused, get behind him and perform the Victory Roll. This causes you to jump on your opponent's shoulders, taking him face-first into the mat. Although it doesn't inflict much damage, it sure is something to show the kiddies.

'Reverse DDT

While a normal DDT is damaging enough, a Reverse DDT is downright deadly. With this move, you get behind your dazed opponent, grab him around the neck, and slam the back of his head to the ground. This move causes a heckuva lot more damage than a Victory Roll.

'Pump Handle Slam

The Pump Handle Slam is another behind-the-opponent move that inflicts just as much damage as the Reverse DDT. It's a variation of the pick-up-your-foe-and-slam-him-to-the-ground, which is indeed what wrestling is all about.

'Monkey Flip

With your opponent up against the turnbuckle, the Monkey Flip causes you to roll him over the top of you and onto the ground, flat on his back. Believe it or not, this move causes plenty o' damage (at least 5) and is a useful attack when in the corner.

'Cobra Clutch

As the name implies, this baby is a hold and quite the hold it is! It doles out a bit of damage and usually is fairly easy to execute, plus it takes a while to finish, giving you a bit of extra time to recuperate.

'Texas Cloverleaf

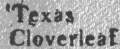

This favorite of the Texas natives is an excellent hold because it inflicts hurt on your enemy while giving you time to recover. Whenever your opponent is on the ground, don't be afraid to twist things to your advantage.

'Choke Slam

Not many moves cause more damage than the Choke Slam (9 points). If you manage to get your opponent by the neck in a Tieup, this move will send him to the ground fast!

Chapter 2

The Modes of Play

There's more to WWF War Zone than a simple Challenge Mode. We have training, weapons, and we even have a steel cage, all of which come with their quirks and quandaries. If you want a few pointers, look no further than the next few pages to learn more.

Training Mode

"Training?" you say, "I don't need no steenkin' training!" And then you went toe-to-toe with the likes of the British Bulldog, who easily mopped the mat with your confused face. If you know what's good for you, you'll train long and hard before making your WWF debut. After all, you don't want to be just another speed bump on a wrestler's way to the IC Championship belt, now do you? You want to be a contender, and the only way you're going to do that is by training, mastering the moves for each wrestler, and practice, practice, practice!

Some words of advice: Don't think that every key combination is the same for each wrestler. Although a lot of moves are repeated from fighter to fighter, the moves for a Belly Belly Suplex for one wrestler may be a Samoan Drop for another. Pay attention to what you're doing, and you'll be in trouble fast!

Also, don't forget about the Free For All Mode, which allows you to use all the moves you've mastered and practiced in combination. In this mode, you can see exactly what you're doing and how you just pulled off the stunning Atomic Drop that waylaid your enemy.

You'll also want to pay special attention to how to perform special holds once you've managed to stun your opponent with all these new moves. There's no sense letting your opponent lie on the mat recuperating while you twiddle your thumbs waiting. When his meter's blue, it's time to dish out some serious pain!

The Challenge

The Challenge is the essence of **WWF War Zone**. This is where you take your chosen superstar and climb, beat, and pummel your way to the king of the ring—the Intercontinental Champion, belt and all! As a rookie, you'll start out at the bottom and work your way up with each victory. Also, other com-

puterized opponents will shuffle around in their rankings as well, so things never stay the same. This is what all that training has been for, but no one ever went into battle without getting a few pointers first. So take heed of the fast and furious tips that follow and use them on those who challenge you.

Challenge Tips

- Don't stand around waiting for something to happen unless you have the weakest of wrestlers. You need to be the aggressor, so get in there and mix it up.

- Avoid getting thrown out of the ring at all costs. While it may be fun to scuffle on the apron, it puts you at serious risk for losing the match by being out of the ring. If you find yourself in that situation, get back in the ring fast.

- While some moves definitely look cooler than others, you should stick with combinations that dole out at least 5 points of damage or more. The only exceptions to this rule are the Punch and Quick Kick, which help throw your opponent temporarily off balance.

- Master the Holds. It doesn't make a whole lot of sense to leave your opponent stunned on the mat while you wait for him to recover. If you can get him in a killer hold, then you seriously increase the odds of defeating him.

- Along those same lines, you also need to know the moves that can really cause the hurtin' when your foe is stunned on the ground. Learn such moves as the Kamikaze Headbutt to give you even more ammunition to take down an opponent.

- Don't attempt to pin your opponent unless you've been dishing out quite a beating for a while. If you try to, you'll just waste precious time that you could be using to inflict even more damage with Holds or drop moves. Better yet, climb up the turnbuckle and really pound on him.

- Speaking of turnbuckles, do your best to whip your opponent into one. While he's stunned in the corner, run over and get in a few quick blows.

- Also, you can use the ropes to your advantage by whipping your opponent into them, and then performing a clothesline on his way back.

- If you find that you may be somewhat out-matched by a bigger opponent (especially Faarooq), try to stay in the center of the ring. This tactic prevents your opponent from throwing you out of the ring, which is a favorite move.

- Master the "Secret Moves" because they almost always offer the most pain for your gain.

- Play to a wrestler's strengths. That's where knowing things such as his height and ratings is so critical (refer to Chapter 3). If your character has no toughness but a lot of speed, you'll have to dance quite a bit to keep him from getting hit. Plus, you'll have to keep moving to get behind your opponent to carry out your own special moves.

Tag Team

Tag Team is monster WWF pandemonium at its finest, and you no doubt want to pair your favorite fighters to see if they have what it takes to beat on any up-and-comers. Essentially, you'll be fighting mano-a-mano as each player takes his turn in spreading the misery. However, this being the WWF, things aren't exactly as orderly as one would like, and so you must be prepared for anything.

Tag Team Tips

- Concentrate on the moves you mastered for your chosen wrestlers. Everything is still the same here, except that you're playing with two, and not one, fighter.

- The wrestlers in the WWF aren't the fairest of fighters, and when an opportunity arises to help out their fellow man, they'll grab it by the throat won't let it pass them by. You need to avoid getting too close to your opponent's partner outside the ring. He'll probably have no qualms about reaching in and pounding you if you get within arm's reach.

- The toughest part about Tag Team is ensuring that you're controlling the correct player. Get real familiar with the "toggle between opponents" button, because it will help you out of a sticky situation fast.

- If you find yourself taking quite a beating, you should "tag up" or at least call for the other player. While you're at it with both of you in the ring, why not get in a few cheap shots?

- The same concepts about staying in the ring in Challenge Mode apply here. If one of your characters gets on the apron, controlling the match becomes much tougher. Stay in the ring at all costs; although having the chance to pound a chair over your opponent's head sounds like fun, it isn't worth losing the match for.

Cage Mode

Time to put the animals of the WWF in the cage where they belong. In the cage, you can run but you can't hide. There's no leaving the ring for a quick breather, and you can't leave until you've thoroughly beat the stuffin' out of the enemy. Again, many of the moves you mastered in Training and Challenge Mode apply here, but with the Cage some things do indeed change.

Cage Mode Tips

- The Whip move can be your best friend, because instead of merely throwing your opponent into the ropes, you're driving his ugly mug into cold, hard steel.

- Keep in mind that your opponent is looking to drive you into the steel bars that make up the cage as well, so stay in the center of the ring as much as possible.

- Don't attempt to climb out of the cage until you're sure your opponent is all but finished. Falling off the sides of the cage or getting knocked down while making your climb can be hazardous to your health.

- Although aerial attacks can be fun, you don't want to miss your target. Not only does it cause a world of hurt, you'll end up looking like a moron!

- Look at the cage as a weapon and not as a hindrance. Perform plenty of throws into the cage to cause double the damage, as the cage breaks your foe's fall.

Weapons Mode

No one ever said fighting in the WWF was fair, and to give it that extra bite, you can use weapons to pummel your opponents. Whether it be a 2X4, a chair, or even a TV set, there's plenty of painful props to pound your foes with. However, you should keep the following few pointers in mind.

Weapons Mode Tips

- Use the Tieup button to grab a weapon and the Punch button to use it.

- Although you do have weapons at your disposal, this is a wrestling match. Grabbing and using a weapon takes a long time, so only pick up a weapon if you've stunned your opponent.

- If your opponent grabs a weapon, don't run, just quickly kick or punch him to knock it out of his hands.

- When your opponent is stunned, don't wait for him to get up before you use your weapon. Use it while he's still on the ground, because he won't be able to knock it out of your hands.

- Wondering what that yellow plate thing is or that gray object on the mat? Don't worry about it! Whatever it is, it hurts when it comes in contact with your opponent's noggin', so pick it up and start the beatings.

- Now's not a good time to climb a turnbuckle and jump on your opponent. That just gives him the time he needs to pick up a 2X4 and knock you out of the ring.

Chapter 3

Know Your Wrestler: All the Right Moves

You ain't nothin' in the WWF if you ain't got the moves, baby. You might be able to bench-press a Buick, but if you don't know how to do the simplest of suplexes, the competition's gonna wipe the mat with your sorry hide.

In this chapter you'll get up close and personal with the game's stars, and discover what makes them tick, and what moves lead them to victory. If you want to see your favorite fighter go all the way, you're gonna have to master his moves. And don't go thinkin' that everyone's got the same moves with different names. Both Steve Austin and Mankind have Front Backbreakers in their little bag o' tricks, but the key combinations are completely different from one another.

A couple of notes on the move lists: The number in the first column (next to every move) indicates the damage that it inflicts. You'll also notice that sometimes you'll see the same move but with a different key combination. Just like there are several ways to skin a cat, there are several ways to do the same move.

Lastly are the key combinations themselves. Because this is 3D, using expressions like "Toward" and "Away" for directions doesn't make a whole lot of sense. To keep things simple, we're gonna stick with "Left" or "Right," "Up" or "Down," and so on, and so on.

LOOKIN' FOR SECRET MOVES? EACH CHARACTER HAS HIS OWN SET OF SECRET MOVES, WHICH ARE HIGHLIGHTED IN RED. SO, IF YOU WANT TO WIN THE CHAMPIONSHIP BELT, MASTER YOUR FAVORITE CHARACTER'S SECRET MOVES!

So, what're you doin' reading this intro already? Let's get to wrestlin!

"Stone Cold" Steve Austin

"Stone Cold" Steve Austin is probably the one every aspiring wrestling champion picks to go all the way, but a quick look at his stats show that his bark is far worse than his bite. When compared to your typical couch potato he's tough, but matched up against a sturdier foe like The Undertaker, he could drop like a stone. However, Austin's got the crowd on his side, plus a few killer moves that will have the competition thinkin' you really are the six million dollar man.

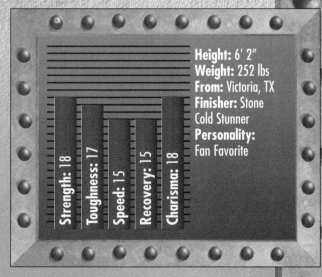

Height: 6' 2"
Weight: 252 lbs
From: Victoria, TX
Finisher: Stone Cold Stunner
Personality: Fan Favorite

Strength: 18
Toughness: 17
Speed: 15
Recovery: 15
Charisma: 18

Behind Opponent

DAMAGE	NAME	MOVE
6	Cobra Clutch	Kick
6	Cobra Clutch	Punch
6	Cobra Clutch	Tieup
7	Pump Handle Slam	Left, Right, Kick or Right, Left, Kick
7	Pump Handle Slam	Up, Down, Kick or Down, Up, Kick
7	Side Slam	Left, Left, Punch or Right, Right, Punch
7	Side Slam	Up, Up, Punch or Down, Down, Punch
8	Reverse DDT	Left, Right, Down Tieup or Right, Left, Down, Tieup

Tieup

DAMAGE	NAME	MOVE
1	Hammerlock	Kick
2	Back Breaker	Punch
3	Fisherman's Suplex	Tieup
4	Inverted Atomic Drop	Left, Kick or Right Kick

DAMAGE	NAME	MOVE
4	Inverted Atomic Drop	Up, Kick or Down, Kick
5	DDT	Left, Punch or Right, Punch
5	DDT	Up, Punch or Down, Punch
6	Overhead Belly Belly Suplex	Left, Tieup or Right, Tieup
6	Overhead Belly Belly Suplex	Up, Tieup or Down, Tieup
7	Vertical Suplex	Left, Up, Kick or Right, Up, Kick
8	Brainbuster	Left, Right, Punch or Right, Left, Punch
9	Power Bomb	Left, Up, Tieup or Right, Up, Tieup
9	Stone Cold Stunner	Left, Left, Tieup or Right, Right, Tieup

Corner (Facing)

DAMAGE	NAME	MOVE
3	Kick In Corner	Kick
1	Climb and Pummel	Punch (Repeating)
1	Repeated Elbows	Tieup (Repeating)
5	Belly Belly Suplex	Left, Left, Kick or Right, Right Kick
5	Belly Belly Suplex	Up, Up, Kick or Down, Down, Kick

DAMAGE	NAME	MOVE
5	Belly Belly Suplex	Left, Left, Punch or Right, Right, Punch
5	Belly Belly Suplex	Up, Up, Punch or Down, Down, Punch
5	Top Rope Superplex	Left, Left, Tieup or Right, Right, Tieup
5	Top Rope Superplex	Up, Up, Tieup or Down, Down, Tieup

Corner (Behind)

DAMAGE	NAME	MOVE
1	Head into Turnbuckle	Kick (Repeating)
1	Head into Turnbuckle	Punch (Repeating)
1	Head into Turnbuckle	Tieup (Repeating)
5	Pump Handle Slam	Left, Tieup or Right, Tieup
5	Pump Handle Slam	Up, Tieup or Down, Tieup

Corner (Running)

DAMAGE	NAME	MOVE
3	Charging Clothesline	Kick
3	Charging Clothesline	Punch
3	Charging Clothesline	Tieup

Ready

| --- | --- | --- |
2	Arm Wrench	Left, Left, Punch or Right, Right, Punch
6	Overhead Belly Belly Suplex	Left, Right, Tieup or Right, Left, Tieup
5	Body Slam	Left, Down, Punch or Right, Down, Punch
4	Clothesline	Up, Up, Punch or Down, Down, Punch
5	Cobra Clutch	Left, Up, Tieup or Right, Up, Tieup
7	DDT	Left, Down, Kick or Right, Down, Kick
6	Front Backbreaker	Left, Down, Tieup or Right, Down, Tieup
6	Gut Wrench	Left, Right, Punch or Right, Left, Punch
2	Hammerlock	Left, Left, Tieup or Right, Right, Tieup
6	Side Belly Belly Suplex	Up, Up, Kick or Down, Down, Kick
6	Samoan Drop	Left, Up, Punch or Right, Up, Punch
5	Short Arm Clothesline	Left, Left, Kick or Right, Right Kick
6	Single Arm DDT	Left, Up, Kick or Right, Up, Kick
6	Spinebuster	Up, Down, Kick or Down, Up, Kick

DAMAGE	NAME	MOVE
7	Vertical Suplex	Up, Down, Tieup or Down, Up, Tieup
9	Stone Cold Stunner	Left, Left, Up, Tieup + Block or Right, Right, Up, Tieup + Block

Ground Holds (At Feet)

DAMAGE	NAME	MOVE
5	Step Over Toe Hold	Left, Left, Kick or Right, Right Kick
5	Step Over Toe Hold	Up, Up, Kick or Down, Down, Kick
6	Half Crab	Left, Right, Kick or Right, Left, Kick
6	Texas Cloverleaf	Up, Down, Kick or Down, Up, Kick
7	STF	Up, Down, Up, Kick or Down, Up, Down, Kick

Ground Holds (At Head)

DAMAGE	NAME	MOVE
5	Arm Wrench	Left, Left, Punch or Right, Right, Punch
5	Arm Wrench	Up, Up, Punch or Down, Down, Punch
6	Rear Chin Lock	Left, Right, Punch or Right, Left, Punch

25

DAMAGE	NAME	MOVE
6	Reverse Chin Lock	Up, Down, Punch or Down, Up, Punch
7	Painkiller	Left, Up, Down, Punch or Right, Down, Up, Punch

Ground Hits (Standing)

DAMAGE	NAME	MOVE
3	Leg Drop (at side)	Kick
1	Stomp	Kick
3	Falling Headbutt	Down, Kick
2	Fist Drop	Punch
1	Driving Elbow Smash	Down, Punch (Repeating Punch)

Ground Hits (Running)

DAMAGE	NAME	MOVE
4	Leg Drop (at side)	Kick
3	Running Elbow Drop	Kick
3	Front Elbow	Punch
3	Front Elbow	Tieup

Running Opponent

DAMAGE	NAME	MOVE
6	Back Body Drop	Kick
4	Clothesline	Punch
2	Arm Drag	Tieup
7	Power Slam	Up, Tieup or Down, Tieup

Kicks/Punches

DAMAGE	NAME	MOVE
2	Quick Kick	Kick
3	Kick	Left, Kick or Right, Kick
3	Kick	Up, Kick or Down, Kick
2	Punch	Punch
2	Inside Forearm	Left, Punch or Right, Punch
5	Haymaker	Up, Punch or Down, Punch

Running

DAMAGE	NAME	MOVE
5	Clothesline Running	Kick
5	Clothesline Running	Tieup
7	Vertical Body Press	Punch

Turnbuckle (Opponent On Ground)

DAMAGE	NAME	MOVE
6	Fist Drop	Kick
6	Fist Drop	Punch
6	Fist Drop	Tieup
7	Double Foot Stomp	Kick + Block
7	Driving Elbow	Punch + Tieup
8	Splash	Left, Left, Punch + Kick or Right, Right, Punch + Kick

Turnbuckle (Opponent Standing)

DAMAGE	NAME	MOVE
6	Bionic Elbow	Kick
6	Bionic Elbow	Punch
6	Bionic Elbow	Tieup
7	Clothesline Turnbuckle	Punch + Tieup
7	Forearm Smash	Kick + Block
8	Shoulder Tackle	Left, Up, Tieup + Block or Right, Up, Tieup + Block

Apron (Opponent On Ground)

DAMAGE	NAME	MOVE
6	**Fist Drop**	**Kick**
6	**Fist Drop**	**Punch**
6	**Fist Drop**	**Tieup**
7	**Double Foot Stomp**	**Kick + Block**
7	**Driving Elbow**	**Punch + Tieup**

Apron (Opponent Standing)

DAMAGE	NAME	MOVE
6	**Bionic Elbow**	**Kick**
6	**Bionic Elbow**	**Punch**
6	**Bionic Elbow**	**Tieup**
7	**Clothesline Apron**	**Punch + Tieup**
7	**Forearm Smash**	**Kick + Block**

British Bulldog

Who knew the English had such fight in them? Bulldog's greatest assets are his tremendous strength and toughness, which compensate for his average height. This gives him a fighting chance against the mightiest of foes. Bulldog comes with a couple of pretty unique moves as well, like the Bearhug and the Gorilla Dress Slam, so don't be afraid to use 'em on unsuspecting opponents.

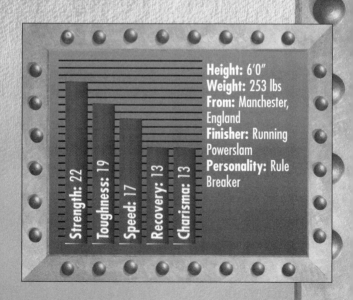

Strength: 22
Toughness: 19
Speed: 17
Recovery: 13
Charisma: 13

Height: 6'0"
Weight: 253 lbs
From: Manchester, England
Finisher: Running Powerslam
Personality: Rule Breaker

Behind Opponent

DAMAGE	NAME	MOVE
6	Russian Leg Sweep	Kick
6	Russian Leg Sweep	Punch
6	Russian Leg Sweep	Tieup
7	Atomic Drop	Left, Left, Kick or Right, Right Kick
7	Atomic Drop	Up, Up, Kick or Down, Down, Kick
7	Atomic Drop	Left, Left, Punch or Right, Right, Punch
7	Atomic Drop	Up, Up, Punch or Down, Down, Punch
3	Victory Roll	Left, Left, Tieup or Right, Right, Tieup
3	Victory Roll	Up, Up, Tieup or Down, Down, Tieup
8	Belly Back Suplex	Left, Up, Right, Tieup or Right, Up, Left, Tieup

Tieup

DAMAGE	NAME	MOVE
1	Hiptoss	Kick
2	Top Wristlock	Punch
3	Chest Breaker	Tieup
4	Fisherman's Suplex	Left, Kick or Right, Kick

DAMAGE	NAME	MOVE
4	Fisherman's Suplex	Up, Kick or Down, Kick
5	Gut Wrench Power Bomb	Left, Punch or Right, Punch
5	Gut Wrench Power Bomb	Up, Punch or Down, Punch
6	Samoan Drop	Left, Tieup or Right, Tieup
6	Samoan Drop	Up, Tieup or Down, Tieup
7	Overhead Belly Belly Suplex	Left, Right, Kick or Right, Left, Kick
8	Double Underhook Suplex	Left, Down, Punch or Right, Down, Punch
9	Hanging Vertical Suplex	Left, Up, Tieup or Right, Up, Tieup
9	Charging Powerslam	Up, Down, Tieup or Down, Up, Tieup

Corner (Facing)

DAMAGE	NAME	MOVE
3	Kick to Ribs	Kick
1	Climb and Pummel	Punch (Repeating)
1	Slap Face	Tieup (Repeating)
5	Oklahoma Stampede	Left, Left, Kick or Right, Right Kick

DAMAGE	NAME	MOVE
5	Oklahoma Stampede	Up, Up, Kick or Down, Down, Kick
5	Belly Belly Suplex	Left, Left, Punch or Right, Right, Punch
5	Belly Belly Suplex	Up, Up, Punch or Down, Down, Punch
5	Superplex	Left, Left, Tieup or Right, Right, Tieup
5	Superplex	Up, Up, Tieup or Down, Down, Tieup
6	Top Rope Superplex	Up, Down, Left, Kick or Down, Up, Right, Kick

Corner (Behind)

DAMAGE	NAME	MOVE
1	Head into Turnbuckle	Kick (Repeating)
1	Head into Turnbuckle	Punch (Repeating)
1	Head into Turnbuckle	Tieup (Repeating)
5	Pump and Slam	Left, Tieup or Right, Tieup
5	Pump and Slam	Up, Tieup or Down, Tieup

Corner (Running)

DAMAGE	NAME	MOVE
3	Charging Clothesline	Kick
3	Charging Clothesline	Punch
3	Charging Clothesline	Tieup

DAMAGE	NAME	MOVE
3	Arm Drag	Down, Down, Punch
2	Arm Wrench	Left, Left, Punch or Right, Right, Punch
5	Bearhug	Up, Down, Punch or Down, Up, Punch
5	Body Slam	Left, Down, Tieup or Right, Down, Tieup
9	Charging Powerslam	Up, Down, Up, Punch + Tieup or Down, Up, Down, Punch + Tieup
6	Overhead Belly Belly Suplex	Left, Right, Tieup or Right, Left, Tieup
3	Crucifix	Left, Up, Kick or Right, Up, Kick
4	Fireman's Carry	Down, Down, Kick
8	Gorilla Dress Slam	Up, Up, Down, Tieup or Down, Down, Up, Tieup
8	Hanging Vertical Suplex	Down, Up, Up, Punch
3	Hiptoss	Up, Up, Kick
6	Samoan Drop	Left, Up, Punch or Right, Up, Punch
1	Small Package	Up, Up, Tieup or Down, Down, Tieup
5	Snap Mare	Left, Down, Kick or Right, Down, Kick

Ground Hold (At Feet)

DAMAGE	NAME	MOVE
5	Spinning Toe Hold	Left, Left, Kick or Right, Right Kick
5	Spinning Toe Hold	Up, Up, Kick or Down, Down, Kick
6	Leg Grapevine	Left, Right, Kick or Right, Left, Kick
6	Texas Cloverleaf	Up, Down, Kick or Down, Up, Kick
7	Boston Crab	Left, Down, Right, Kick or Right, Down, Left, Kick

Ground Holds (At Head)

DAMAGE	NAME	MOVE
5	Arm Wrench	Left, Left, Punch or Right, Right, Punch
5	Arm Wrench	Up, Up, Punch or Down, Down, Punch
6	Rear Chin Lock	Left, Right, Punch or Right, Left, Punch
6	Stump Puller	Up, Down, Punch or Down, Up, Punch
7	Camel Clutch	Left, Up, Right, Punch or Right, Up, Left, Punch

Ground Hits (Standing)

DAMAGE	NAME	MOVE
1	Stomp	Kick
3	Double Foot Stomp	Down, Kick
2	Elbow Drop	Punch

Ground Hits (Running)

DAMAGE	NAME	MOVE
3	Running Knee Drop	Kick
3	Running Knee Drop	Tieup
3	Running Elbow Drop	Punch

Running Opponent

DAMAGE	NAME	MOVE
5	Drop Kick	Kick
5	Clothesline	Punch
5	Arm Drag	Tieup
7	Power Slam	Up, Tieup or Down, Tieup

Kicks/Punches

DAMAGE	NAME	MOVE
2	Quick Kick	Kick
5	Drop Kick	Up, Kick
2	Punch	Punch
3	European Uppercut	Up, Punch or Down, Punch
2	Forearm	Left, Punch or Right, Punch

Running

DAMAGE	NAME	MOVE
6	Flying Shoulder Tackle	Kick
5	Clothesline Running	Punch
5	Spinning Neck Breaker	Tieup
3	Crucifix	Punch + Tieup

Turnbuckle (Opponent On Ground)

DAMAGE	NAME	MOVE
6	Knee Drop	Kick
6	Knee Drop	Punch
6	Knee Drop	Tieup

DAMAGE	NAME	MOVE
7	Kamikaze Headbutt	Punch + Tieup
7	Splash	Kick + Block
8	Somersault Senton Splash	Up, Up, Punch + Kick

Turnbuckle (Opponent Standing)

DAMAGE	NAME	MOVE
6	Torpedo Drop Kick	Kick
6	Torpedo Drop Kick	Punch
6	Torpedo Drop Kick	Tieup
7	Body Press	Kick + Block
3	Sunset Flip (in front of opponent)	Punch + Tieup
6	Torpedo Drop Kick	Punch + Tieup
8	Clothesline Turnbuckle	Left, Right, Tieup + Block or Right, Left, Tieup + Block

Apron (Opponent On Ground)

DAMAGE	NAME	MOVE
6	Knee Drop	Kick
6	Knee Drop	Punch
6	Knee Drop	Tieup
7	Kamikaze Headbutt	Punch + Tieup
7	Splash	Kick + Block

Apron (Opponent Standing)

DAMAGE	NAME	MOVE
6	Torpedo Drop Kick	Kick
6	Torpedo Drop Kick	Punch
6	Torpedo Drop Kick	Kick
7	Body Press	Kick + Block
7	Body Press	Punch + Tieup

Faarooq

What Faarooq lacks in speed and charisma, he definitely makes up for in strength and toughness. While he is indeed a fan favorite, with such a low charisma rating you can't depend on the crowd to get Faarooq's adrenaline pumping. His Power Bomb and Secret Dominator move will bring nearly any opponent to his knees, as will his Brainbuster and Belly Back Suplex. Be Warned: When fighting against the CPU version of Faarooq, he will attempt to throw you out of the ring at the first possible opportunity!

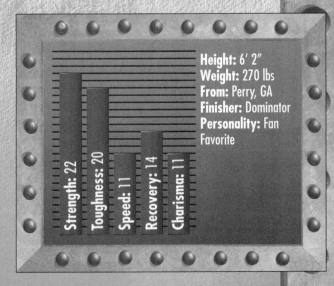

Strength: 22
Toughness: 20
Speed: 11
Recovery: 14
Charisma: 11

Height: 6' 2"
Weight: 270 lbs
From: Perry, GA
Finisher: Dominator
Personality: Fan Favorite

Behind Opponent

DAMAGE	NAME	MOVE
6	Full Nelson	Kick
6	Full Nelson	Punch
6	Full Nelson	Tieup
7	Atomic Drop	Left, Left, Kick or Right, Right Kick
7	Atomic Drop	Up, Up, Kick or Down, Down, Kick
7	Atomic Drop	Left, Left, Punch or Right, Right, Punch
7	Atomic Drop	Up, Up, Punch or Down, Down, Punch
8	Belly Back Suplex	Left, Up, Right, Tieup or Right, Up, Left, Tieup

Tieup

DAMAGE	NAME	MOVE
1	Hiptoss	Kick
2	Chest Breaker	Punch
3	Side Slam	Tieup
4	Gut Wrench Power Bomb	Left, Kick or Right Kick
4	Gut Wrench Power Bomb	Up, Kick or Down, Kick
5	Side Belly Belly Suplex	Left Punch or Right Punch
5	Side Belly Belly Suplex	Up Punch or Down Punch

DAMAGE	NAME	MOVE
6	Northern Lights Suplex	Left, Tieup or Right, Tieup
6	Northern Lights Suplex	Up, Tieup or Down, Tieup
7	Sidewalk Slam	Up, Down, Kick or Down, Up, Kick
8	Brainbuster	Left, Right, Punch or Right, Left, Punch
9	Power Bomb	Up, Left, Tieup or Down, Right, Tieup

Corner (Facing)

DAMAGE	NAME	MOVE
3	Choke with Boot	Kick
1	Charging Shoulder	Punch (Repeating)
1	Charging Shoulder	Tieup (Repeating)
5	Overhead Press	Left, Left, Kick or Right, Right Kick
5	Overhead Press	Up, Up, Kick or Down, Down, Kick
5	Superplex	Left, Left, Punch or Right, Right, Punch
5	Superplex	Up, Up, Punch or Down, Down, Punch
5	Top Rope Superplex	Left, Left, Tieup or Right, Right, Tieup
5	Top Rope Superplex	Up, Up, Tieup or Down, Down, Tieup

Corner (Behind)

DAMAGE	NAME	MOVE
1	Head into Turnbuckle	Kick (Repeating)
1	Head into Turnbuckle	Punch (Repeating)
1	Head into Turnbuckle	Tieup (Repeating)
5	Pump Handle Slam	Left, Tieup or Right, Tieup
5	Pump Handle Slam	Up, Tieup or Down, Tieup

Corner (Running)

DAMAGE	NAME	MOVE
3	Charging Clothesline	Kick
3	Charging Clothesline	Punch
3	Charging Clothesline	Tieup

Ready

DAMAGE	NAME	MOVE
5	Bearhug	Left, Down, Punch or Right, Down, Punch
9	Dominator	Up, Up, Up, Tieup + Block
3	Hiptoss	Up, Up, Kick
2	Japanese Arm Drag	Down, Down, Punch

DAMAGE	NAME	MOVE
4	Knee to Face	Left, Down, Kick or Right, Down, Kick
8	Press Slam	Down, Down, Left, Tieup or Down, Down, Right, Tieup
6	Side Belly Belly Suplex	Left, Up, Kick or Right, Up, Kick
5	Short Arm Clothesline	Up, Down, Punch or Down, Up, Punch
6	Shoulder Breaker	Left, Right, Punch or Right, Left, Punch
7	Sidewalk Slam	Left, Right, Kick or Right, Left, Kick
6	Spinebuster	Up, Down, Kick or Down, Up, Kick
5	Spinning Neck Breaker	Left, Right, Tieup or Right, Left, Tieup
8	Choke Slam	Left, Left, Up, Punch or Right, Right, Up, Punch
7	Vertical Suplex	Left, Up, Tieup or Right, Up, Tieup

Ground Holds (At Feet)

DAMAGE	NAME	MOVE
5	Knee to Inside Leg	Left, Left, Kick or Right, Right Kick
5	Knee to Inside Leg	Up, Up, Kick or Down, Down, Kick

DAMAGE	NAME	MOVE
6	Elbow to Groin	Left, Right, Kick or Right, Left, Kick
6	Inverted STF	Up, Down, Kick or Down, Up, Kick
7	Boston Crab	Left, Down, Right, Kick or Right, Down, Left, Kick

Ground Holds (At Head)

DAMAGE	NAME	MOVE
5	Arm Wrench	Left, Left, Punch or Right, Right, Punch
5	Arm Wrench	Up, Up, Punch or Down, Down, Punch
6	Knee to Back	Left, Right, Punch or Right, Left, Punch
6	Blatant Choke	Up, Down, Punch or Down, Up, Punch
7	Camel Clutch	Left, Up, Right, Punch or Right, Up, Left, Punch

Ground Hits (Standing)

DAMAGE	NAME	MOVE
1	Stomp	Kick
3	Falling Headbutt	Down, Kick
3	Axhandle Smash	Punch

45

Ground Hits (Running)

DAMAGE	NAME	MOVE
3	Running Knee Drop	Kick
3	Fist Drop	Punch
4	Falling Headbutt	Tieup

Running Opponent

DAMAGE	NAME	MOVE
4	Boot to Face	Kick
5	Clothesline	Punch
7	Power Slam	Tieup
8	Sidewalk Slam	Left Punch or Right Punch

Kicks/Punches

DAMAGE	NAME	MOVE
2	Quick Kick	Kick
3	Kick	Left, Kick or Right Kick
2	Punch	Punch
3	Choke	Up, Punch or Down, Punch
2	Forearm	Left, Punch or Right, Punch

Running

DAMAGE	NAME	MOVE
6	Flying Shoulder Tackle	Kick
5	Clothesline Running	Punch
6	Flying Shoulder Tackle	Tieup

Turnbuckle (Opponent On Ground)

DAMAGE	NAME	MOVE
6	Fist Drop	Kick
6	Fist Drop	Punch
6	Fist Drop	Tieup
7	Knee Drop	Kick + Block
7	Driving Elbow	Punch + Tieup
8	Double Foot Stomp	Up, Left, Punch + Kick or Up, Right, Punch + Kick

Turnbuckle (Opponent Standing)

DAMAGE	NAME	MOVE
6	Axhandle Smash	Kick
6	Axhandle Smash	Punch

DAMAGE	NAME	MOVE
6	Axhandle Smash	Tieup
7	Forearm Smash	Kick + Block
7	Clothesline Turnbuckle	Punch + Tieup
8	Shoulder Tackle	Left, Up, Tieup + Block or Right, Up, Tieup + Block

Apron (Opponent On Ground)

DAMAGE	NAME	MOVE
6	Fist Drop	Kick
6	Fist Drop	Punch
6	Fist Drop	Tieup
7	Knee Drop	Kick + Block
7	Driving Elbow	Punch + Tieup

Apron (Opponent Standing)

DAMAGE	NAME	MOVE
6	Axhandle Smash	Kick
6	Axhandle Smash	Punch
6	Axhandle Smash	Tieup
7	Forearm Smash	Kick + Block
7	Clothesline Apron	Punch + Tieup

Goldust

With an almost unheard of recovery rating, you don't have to worry about Goldust kissing the mat for too long. Although he's slow compared to some other fighters, once he can grab hold, watch out! His Curtain Call and Piledriver are good as gold in the right hands, turning your fighting foes into dust–gold dust, that is!

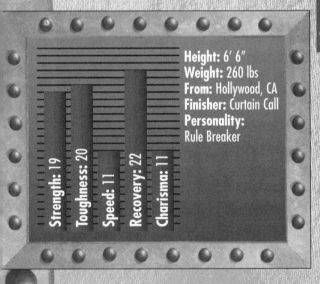

Strength: 19
Toughness: 20
Speed: 11
Recovery: 22
Charisma: 11

Height: 6' 6"
Weight: 260 lbs
From: Hollywood, CA
Finisher: Curtain Call
Personality:
Rule Breaker

Goldust

Behind Opponent

DAMAGE	NAME	MOVE
6	Abdominal Stretch	Kick
6	Abdominal Stretch	Punch
6	Abdominal Stretch	Tieup
7	Atomic Drop	Left, Left, Kick or Right, Right, Kick
7	Atomic Drop	Up, Up, Kick or Down, Down, Kick
7	Atomic Drop	Left, Left, Punch or Right, Right, Punch
7	Atomic Drop	Up, Up, Punch or Down, Down, Punch
8	Reverse DDT	Left, Right, Down, Tieup or Right, Left, Down, Tieup
9	Curtain Call	Left, Down, Down, Tieup + Block or Right, Down, Down, Tieup + Block

Tieup

DAMAGE	NAME	MOVE
1	Hiptoss	Kick
2	Atomic Drop	Punch
3	Inverted Atomic Drop	Tieup

DAMAGE	NAME	MOVE
4	DDT	Left, Kick or Right, Kick
4	DDT	Up, Kick or Down, Kick
5	Vertical Suplex	Left, Punch or Right, Punch
5	Vertical Suplex	Up, Punch or Right, Punch
6	Samoan Drop	Left, Tieup or Right, Tieup
6	Samoan Drop	Up, Tieup or Down, Tieup
7	Brainbuster	Left, Down, Kick or Right, Down, Kick
8	Bulldog	Left, Up, Punch or Right, Up, Punch
9	Piledriver	Up, Down, Tieup or Down, Up, Tieup

Corner (Facing)

DAMAGE	NAME	MOVE
3	Kick in Corner	Kick
1	Chest Chop	Punch (Repeating)
1	Repeated Elbows	Tieup (Repeating)
5	Superplex	Left, Left, Kick or Right, Right, Kick
5	Superplex	Up, Up, Kick or Down, Down, Kick
5	Superplex	Left, Left, Punch or Right, Right, Punch

Goldust

51

DAMAGE	NAME	MOVE
5	Superplex	Up, Up, Punch or Down, Down, Punch
5	Top Rope Superplex	Left, Left, Tieup or Right, Right Tieup
5	Top Rope Superplex	Up, Up, Tieup or Down, Down, Tieup

Corner (Behind)

DAMAGE	NAME	MOVE
1	Head into Turnbuckle	Kick (Repeating)
1	Head into Turnbuckle	Punch (Repeating)
1	Head into Turnbuckle	Tieup (Repeating)
5	Pump Handle Slam	Left, Tieup or Right, Tieup
5	Pump Handle Slam	Up, Tieup or Down, Tieup

Corner (Running)

DAMAGE	NAME	MOVE
3	Charging Clothesline	Kick
3	Charging Clothesline	Punch
3	Charging Clothesline	Tieup

Ready

DAMAGE	NAME	MOVE
4	Abdominal Stretch	Left, Right, Tieup or Right, Left, Tieup
5	Body Slam	Left, Down, Tieup or Right, Down, Tieup
7	DDT	Left, Down, Kick or Right, Down, Kick
6	Gut Wrench	Left, Right, Punch or Right, Left, Punch
3	Hiptoss	Down, Down, Kick
2	Japanese Arm Drag	Down, Down, Punch
4	Kneebreaker	Up, Down, Kick or Down, Up, Kick
5	Neck Breaker	Left, Down, Punch or Right, Down, Punch
6	Samoan Drop	Left, Up, Punch or Right, Up, Punch
6	Single Arm DDT	Left, Up, Kick or Right, Up, Kick
3	Sleeper	Up, Down, Punch or Down, Up, Punch
5	Snap Mare	Left, Up, Tieup or Right, Up, Tieup
7	Vertical Suplex	Up, Down, Tieup or Down, Up, Tieup

Goldust

Ground Holds (At Feet)

DAMAGE	NAME	MOVE
5	Elbow Drop Onto Leg	Left, Left, Kick or Right, Right, Kick
5	Elbow Drop Onto Leg	Up, Up, Kick or Down, Down, Kick
6	Knee to Inside Leg	Left, Right, Kick or Right, Left, Kick
6	Spinning Toe Hold	Up, Down, Kick or Down, Up, Kick
7	Headbutt to Groin	Left, Up, Right, Kick or Right, Up, Left, Kick

Ground Holds (At Head)

DAMAGE	NAME	MOVE
5	Arm Wrench	Left, Left, Punch or Right, Right, Punch
5	Arm Wrench	Up, Up, Punch or Down, Down, Punch
6	Rear Chin Lock	Left, Right, Punch or Right, Left, Punch
6	Stump Puller	Up, Down, Punch or Down, Up, Punch

Ground Hits (Standing)

DAMAGE	NAME	MOVE
3	Leg Drop (At Side)	Kick
1	Stomp	Kick
3	Double Foot Stomp	Down, Kick
2	Fist Drop	Punch

Ground Hits (Running)

DAMAGE	NAME	MOVE
3	Running Knee Drop	Kick
3	Fist Drop	Punch
4	Butt Drop	Tieup

Running Opponent

DAMAGE	NAME	MOVE
5	Drop Kick Against Running	Kick
5	Clothesline	Punch
5	Flying Back Elbow	Tieup
6	Back Body Drop	Up, Punch or Down, Punch

Kicks/Punches

DAMAGE	NAME	MOVE
2	Quick Kick	Kick
3	Kick	Left, Kick or Right, Kick
1	Slap	Punch
3	European Uppercut	Up, Punch or Down, Punch
2	Punch	Left, Punch or Right, Punch

Running

DAMAGE	NAME	MOVE
5	Drop Kick Running	Kick
4	Uppercut from Knees	Tieup
5	Flying Clothesline	Punch

Turnbuckle (Opponent On Ground)

DAMAGE	NAME	MOVE
6	Knee Drop	Kick
6	Knee Drop	Punch
6	Knee Drop	Tieup

DAMAGE	NAME	MOVE
7	Butt Drop	Kick + Block
7	Fist Drop	Punch + Tieup
8	Somersault Senton Splash	Up, Up, Punch + Kick

Turnbuckle (Opponent Standing)

DAMAGE	NAME	MOVE
6	Bionic Elbow	Kick
6	Bionic Elbow	Punch
6	Bionic Elbow	Tieup
7	Forearm Smash	Kick + Block
7	Flying Butt Bump	Punch + Tieup
8	Shoulder Tackle	Left, Up, Tieup + Block or Right, Up, Tieup + Block

Apron (Opponent On Ground)

DAMAGE	NAME	MOVE
6	Knee Drop	Kick
6	Knee Drop	Punch
6	Knee Drop	Tieup
7	Butt Drop	Kick + Block
7	Fist Drop	Punch + Tieup

Apron (Opponent Standing)

DAMAGE	NAME	MOVE
6	Bionic Elbow	Kick
6	Bionic Elbow	Punch
6	Bionic Elbow	Tieup
7	Forearm Smash	Kick + Block
7	Flying Butt Bump	Punch + Tieup

Triple H

Some think the H stands for "Hurt," while others feel it means "Humiliation." Either way, considering Triple H's strength, there will be plenty of both to dish out if you know what you're doing. His Power Bomb and Pedigree moves can also dole out some hopelessness to those foolish enough to meet these moves head on.

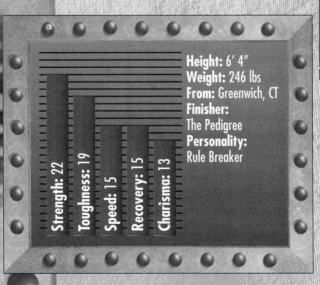

Strength: 22
Toughness: 19
Speed: 15
Recovery: 15
Charisma: 13

Height: 6' 4"
Weight: 246 lbs
From: Greenwich, CT
Finisher: The Pedigree
Personality: Rule Breaker

Behind Opponent

DAMAGE	NAME	MOVE
6	Cobra Clutch	Kick
6	Cobra Clutch	Punch
6	Cobra Clutch	Tieup
7	Atomic Drop	Left, Left, Kick or Right, Right, Kick
7	Atomic Drop	Up, Up, Kick or Down, Down, Kick
7	Pump Handle Slam	Left, Left, Punch or Right, Right, Punch
7	Pump Handle Slam	Up, Up, Punch or Down, Down, Punch
8	Neck Breaker	Left, Up, Up, Tieup or Right, Up, Up, Tieup

Tieup

DAMAGE	NAME	MOVE
1	Hammerlock	Kick
2	Neck Breaker	Punch
3	Shoulder Breaker	Tieup
4	Fisherman's Suplex	Left, Kick or Right, Kick
4	Fisherman's Suplex	Up, Kick, Up, Kick or Down, Kick, Down, Kick
5	Gut Wrench Power Bomb	Left, Punch or Right, Punch

DAMAGE	NAME	MOVE
5	Gut Wrench Power Bomb	Up, Punch or Down, Punch
6	Northern Lights Suplex	Left, Tieup or Right, Tieup
6	Northern Lights Suplex	Up, Tieup or Down, Tieup
7	Overhead Belly Belly Suplex	Left, Up, Kick or Right, Down, Kick
8	Double Underhook Suplex	Up, Down, Punch or Down, Up, Punch
9	Power Bomb	Left, Up, Tieup or Right, Up, Tieup

Corner (Facing)

DAMAGE	NAME	MOVE
3	Choke with Boot	Kick
1	Chest Chop	Punch (Repeating)
1	Charging Shoulder	Tieup (Repeating)
5	Belly Belly	Left, Left, Kick or Right, Right, Kick
5	Belly Belly Suplex	Up, Up, Kick or Down, Down, Kick
5	Superplex	Left, Left, Punch or Right, Right, Punch
5	Superplex	Up, Up, Punch or Down, Down, Punch

Triple H

DAMAGE	NAME	MOVE
5	Top Rope Superplex	Left, Left, Tieup or Right, Right, Tieup
5	Top Rope Superplex	Up, Up, Tieup or Down, Down, Tieup

Corner (Behind)

DAMAGE	NAME	MOVE
1	Head into Turnbuckle	Kick (Repeating)
1	Head into Turnbuckle	Punch (Repeating)
1	Head into Turnbuckle	Tieup (Repeating)
5	Pump Handle Slam	Left, Tieup or Right, Tieup
5	Pump Handle Slam	Up, Tieup or Down, Tieup

Corner (Running)

DAMAGE	NAME	MOVE
3	Avalanche	Kick
3	Avalanche	Punch
3	Avalanche	Tieup

Ready

DAMAGE	NAME	MOVE
2	Arm Wrench	Left, Left, Punch or Right, Right, Punch
6	Overhead Belly Belly Suplex	Left, Right, Tieup or Right, Left, Tieup
5	Clothesline	Left, Down, Punch or Right, Down, Punch
7	DDT	Left, Down, Kick or Right, Down, Kick
3	Drop Toe Hold	Down, Down, Kick
2	Hammerlock	Up, Up, Punch
2	Japanese Arm Drag	Down, Down, Punch
4	Kneebreaker	Left, Up, Kick or Right, Up, Kick
4	Knee to Face	Left, Left, Kick or Right, Right, Kick
5	Neck Breaker	Left, Up, Punch or Right, Up, Punch
9	Pedigree	Left, Down, Right, Punch + Tieup or Right, Down, Punch + Tieup
6	Fisherman's Suplex	Left, Up, Tieup or Right, Up, Tieup
3	Sleeper	Left, Left, Tieup or Right, Right, Tieup
7	Vertical Suplex	Left, Down, Tieup or Right, Down, Tieup

Ground Holds (At Feet)

DAMAGE	NAME	MOVE
5	Step Over Toe Hold	Left, Left, Kick or Right, Right, Kick
5	Step Over Toe Hold	Up, Up, Kick or Down, Down, Kick
6	Half Crab	Left, Right, Kick or Right, Left, Kick
6	Texas Cloverleaf	Up, Down, Kick or Down, Up, Kick
7	Figure Four Leglock	Left, Up, Left, Kick or Right, Down, Right, Kick

Ground Holds (At Head)

DAMAGE	NAME	MOVE
5	Arm Wrench	Left, Left, Punch or Right, Right, Punch
5	Arm Wrench	Up, Up, Punch or Down, Down, Punch
6	Rear Chin Lock	Left, Right, Punch or Right, Left, Punch
6	Knee to Back	Up, Down, Punch or Down, Up Punch
7	Blatant Choke	Left, Down, Right, Punch or Right, Down, Left, Punch

Ground Hits (Standing)

DAMAGE	NAME	MOVE
3	Leg Drop (at side)	Kick
1	Stomp	Kick
2	Fist Drop	Punch
3	Falling Headbutt	Down, Kick

Ground Hits (Running)

DAMAGE	NAME	MOVE
3	Running Knee Drop	Kick
3	Fist Drop	Punch
3	Fist Drop	Tieup

Running Opponent

DAMAGE	NAME	MOVE
3	Drop Toe Hold	Kick
6	Back Body Drop	Punch
5	Flying Back Elbow	Tieup
7	Power Slam	Up, Tieup or Down, Tieup

Kicks/Punches

DAMAGE	NAME	MOVE
2	Quick Kick	Kick
3	Kick	Up, Kick or Down, Kick
3	Grab and Punch	Punch
3	Inside Forearm	Up, Punch or Down, Punch
2	Punch	Left, Punch or Right, Punch

Running

DAMAGE	NAME	MOVE
5	Drop Kick Running	Kick
5	Clothesline Running	Punch
5	Cross Body Block	Tieup

Turnbuckle (Opponent On Ground)

DAMAGE	NAME	MOVE
6	Knee Drop	Kick
6	Knee Drop	Punch
6	Knee Drop	Tieup

DAMAGE	NAME	MOVE
7	Double Foot Stomp	Kick + Block
7	Driving Elbow	Punch + Tieup
8	Somersault Senton Splash	Up, Up, Punch + Kick

Turnbuckle (Opponent Standing)

DAMAGE	NAME	MOVE
6	Axhandle Smash	Kick
6	Axhandle Smash	Punch
6	Axhandle Smash	Tieup
7	Clothesline Turnbuckle	Kick + Block
7	Shoulder Tackle	Punch + Tieup
8	Body Press (in front of opponent)	Up, Left, Tieup + Block or Up, Right, Tieup + Block

Apron (Opponent On Ground)

DAMAGE	NAME	MOVE
6	Knee Drop	Kick
6	Knee Drop	Punch
6	Knee Drop	Tieup
7	Double Foot Stomp	Kick + Block
7	Driving Elbow	Punch + Tieup

Apron (Opponent Standing)

DAMAGE	NAME	MOVE
6	Axhandle Smash	Kick
6	Axhandle Smash	Punch
6	Axhandle Smash	Tieup
7	Clothesline	Kick + Block Apron
7	Shoulder Tackle	Punch + Tieup

Rocky Maivia

It's the rare Rule Breaker who bubbles with personality, and The Rock isn't trying to make any friends (he's a wrestler, not a politician). He's tough and his moves show it, with a Piledriver as deadly as anyone's, not to mention his secret

Rock Bottom move. If you're willing to master his secret moves, there's plenty of hurt there as well, with a Belly Back Suplex and his Laying The Smack Down moves.

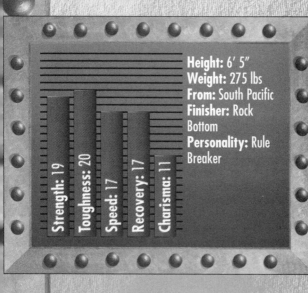

Height: 6' 5"
Weight: 275 lbs
From: South Pacific
Finisher: Rock Bottom
Personality: Rule Breaker

Strength: 19
Toughness: 20
Speed: 17
Recovery: 17
Charisma: 11

Behind Opponent

DAMAGE	NAME	MOVE
6	Cross Face Chicken Wing	Kick
6	Cross Face Chicken Wing	Punch
6	Cross Face Chicken Wing	Tieup
7	Pump Handle Slam	Left, Left, Kick or Right, Right, Kick
7	Pump Handle Slam	Up, Up, Kick or Down, Down, Kick
7	Reverse DDT	Left, Left, Punch or Right, Right, Punch
7	Reverse DDT	Up, Up, Punch or Down, Down, Punch
3	Victory Roll	Left, Left, Tieup or Right, Right, Tieup
3	Victory Roll	Up, Up, Tieup or Down, Down, Tieup
8	Belly Back Suplex	Left, Up, Right, Tieup or Right, Up, Left, Tieup

Tieup

DAMAGE	NAME	MOVE
1	Arm Drag	Kick
2	Shoulder Breaker	Punch
3	DDT	Tieup

DAMAGE	NAME	MOVE
4	Side Belly Belly Suplex	Left, Kick or Right, Kick
4	Side Belly Belly Suplex	Up, Kick or Down, Kick
5	Inverted Atomic Drop	Left, Punch or Right, Punch
5	Inverted Atomic Drop	Up, Punch or Down, Punch
6	Sidewalk Slam	Left, Tieup or Right, Tieup
6	Sidewalk Slam	Up, Tieup or Down, Tieup
7	Double Underhook Suplex	Left, Down, Kick or Right, Down, Kick
8	Brainbuster	Left, Right, Punch or Right, Left, Punch
9	Piledriver	Up, Down, Tieup or Down, Up, Tieup

Corner (Facing)

DAMAGE	NAME	MOVE
3	Choke with Boot	Kick
1	Climb and Pummel	Punch (Repeating)
3	Splash In Corner	Tieup
5	Flying Head Scissors	Left, Left, Kick or Right, Right, Kick

DAMAGE	NAME	MOVE
5	Flying Head Scissors	Up, Up, Kick or Down, Down, Kick
5	Swinging DDT	Left, Left, Punch or Right, Right, Punch
5	Swinging DDT	Up, Up, Punch or Down, Down, Punch
5	Belly Belly Suplex	Left, Left, Tieup or Right, Right, Tieup
5	Belly Belly Suplex	Up, Up, Tieup or Down, Down, Tieup
7	Hurricanranna	Left, Right, Up, Kick or Right, Left, Up, Kick
8	Top Rope Superplex	Left, Up, Right, Punch or Right, Up, Left, Punch

Corner (Behind)

DAMAGE	NAME	MOVE
1	Head into Turnbuckle	Kick (Repeating)
1	Head into Turnbuckle	Punch (Repeating)
1	Head into Turnbuckle	Tieup (Repeating)
5	Pump Handle Slam	Left, Tieup or Right, Tieup
5	Pump Handle Slam	Up, Tieup or Down, Tieup

Corner (Running)

DAMAGE	NAME	MOVE
3	Avalanche	Kick
3	Avalanche	Punch
3	Avalanche	Tieup

Ready

DAMAGE	NAME	MOVE
6	Front Face DDT	Left, Right, Punch or Right, Left, Punch
2	Arm Drag	Up, Up, Punch
3	Drop Toe Hold	Down, Down, Kick
8	Hurricanranna	Left, Right, Up, Kick or Right, Left, Up, Kick
3	Headlock Takedown	Left, Left, Tieup or Right, Right, Tieup
2	Japanese Arm Drag	Down, Down, Punch
6	Overhead Belly Belly Suplex	Left, Up, Tieup or Right, Up, Tieup
6	Samoan Drop	Left, Up, Punch or Right, Up, Punch
6	Side Belly Belly Suplex	Left, Down, Kick or Right, Down, Kick
5	Short Arm Clothesline	Up, Up, Tieup or Down, Down, Tieup
6	Shoulder Breaker	Left, Down, Punch or Right, Down, Punch

DAMAGE	NAME	MOVE
6	Spinebuster	Up, Down, Punch or Down, Up, Punch
8	Laying The Smack Down	Left, Right, Up, Punch or Right, Left, Up, Punch
9	Rock Bottom	Left, Left, Up, Punch + Tieup or Right, Right, Up, Punch + Tieup

Ground Holds (Feet)

DAMAGE	NAME	MOVE
5	Elbow Drop Onto Leg	Left, Left, Kick or Right, Right, Kick
5	Elbow Drop Onto Leg	Up, Up, Kick or Down, Down, Kick
6	Spinning Toe Hold	Left, Right, Kick or Right, Left, Kick
6	Inverted STF	Up, Down, Kick or Down, Up, Kick
7	STF	Up, Down, Down, Kick or Down, Up, Up, Kick

Ground Holds (Head)

DAMAGE	NAME	MOVE
5	Arm Wrench	Left, Left, Punch or Right, Right, Punch

DAMAGE	NAME	MOVE
5	Arm Wrench	Up, Up, Punch or Down, Down, Punch
6	Reverse Chin Lock	Left, Right, Punch or Right, Left, Punch
6	Short Arm Scissor	Up, Down, Punch or Down, Up, Punch

Ground Hits (Standing)

DAMAGE	NAME	MOVE
3	Leg Drop (at side)	Kick
1	Stomp	Kick
3	Falling Headbutt	Down, Kick
4	Splash	Down, Punch
2	Fist Drop	Punch

Ground Hits (Running)

DAMAGE	NAME	MOVE
4	Leg Drop (at side)	Kick
3	Running Knee Drop	Kick
3	Running Knee Drop	Punch
4	Splash	Tieup

Running Opponent

DAMAGE	NAME	MOVE
5	Drop Kick	Kick
6	Back Body Drop	Punch
7	Power Slam	Tieup
8	Hurricanranna	Up, Kick or Down, Kick

Kicks/Punches

DAMAGE	NAME	MOVE
4	Standing Jump Kick	Kick
5	Drop Kick	Up, Kick
2	Punch	Punch
3	Discus Punch	Left, Punch or Right, Punch
3	Discus Punch	Up, Punch or Down, Punch

Running

DAMAGE	NAME	MOVE
5	Drop Kick Running	Kick
5	Flying Clothesline	Punch
3	Crucifix	Tieup
8	Hurricanranna	Punch + Tieup

Turnbuckle (Opponent On Ground)

DAMAGE	NAME	MOVE
6	Elbow Drop	Kick
6	Elbow Drop	Punch
6	Elbow Drop	Tieup
7	Fist Drop	Punch + Tieup
7	Knee Drop	Kick + Block
8	Splash	Left, Left, Punch + Kick or Right, Right, Punch + Kick

Turnbuckle (Opponent Standing)

DAMAGE	NAME	MOVE
6	Drop Kick Turnbuckle	Kick
6	Drop Kick Turnbuckle	Punch
6	Drop Kick Turnbuckle	Tieup
7	Clothesline Turnbuckle	Kick + Block
7	Shoulder Tackle	Punch + Tieup
8	Body Press (in front of opponent)	Up, Left, Tieup + Block or Up, Right, Tieup + Block

Apron (Opponent On Ground)

DAMAGE	NAME	MOVE
6	Elbow Drop	Kick
6	Elbow Drop	Punch
6	Elbow Drop	Tieup
7	Knee Drop	Kick + Block
7	Fist Drop	Punch + Tieup

Apron (Opponent Standing)

DAMAGE	NAME	MOVE
6	Drop Kick Apron	Kick
6	Drop Kick Apron	Punch
6	Drop Kick Apron	Tieup
7	Clothesline Apron	Kick + Block
7	Shoulder Tackle	Punch + Tieup

Mankind

Mankind may look like a freak, but he isn't a pushover. With a near perfect toughness rating and an excellent recovery stat, those steppin' into the ring with this Rule Breaker need to worry about being broken. His finishing move, the Mandible Claw, is as deadly as his Piledriver. Plus,

Mankind's Somersault Senton Splash isn't anything to sneeze at either, especially considering his ability to withstand the mightiest of blows.

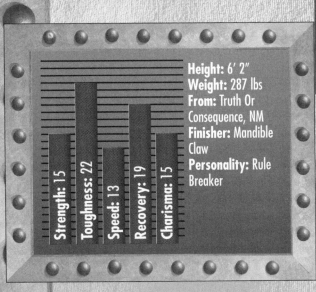

Height: 6' 2"
Weight: 287 lbs
From: Truth Or Consequence, NM
Finisher: Mandible Claw
Personality: Rule Breaker

Strength: 15
Toughness: 22
Speed: 13
Recovery: 19
Charisma: 15

Mankind

Behind Opponent

DAMAGE	NAME	MOVE
6	Nerve Hold	Kick
6	Nerve Hold	Punch
6	Nerve Hold	Tieup
7	Cross Face Chicken Wing	Left, Left, Kick or Right, Right, Kick
7	Cross Face Chicken Wing	Up, Up, Kick or Down, Down, Kick
7	Reverse DDT	Left, Left, Punch or Right, Right, Punch
7	Reverse DDT	Up, Up, Punch or Down, Down, Punch
8	Side Slam	Left, Left, Up, Tieup or Right, Right, Up, Tieup

Tieup

DAMAGE	NAME	MOVE
1	Hiptoss	Kick
2	DDT	Punch
3	Side Belly Belly Suplex	Tieup
4	Samoan Drop	Left, Kick or Right, Kick
4	Samoan Drop	Up, Kick or Down, Kick
5	Inverted Atomic Drop	Left, Punch or Right, Punch

Chapter 8

DAMAGE	NAME	MOVE
5	Inverted Atomic Drop	Up, Punch or Down, Punch
6	Vertical Suplex	Left, Tieup or Right, Tieup
6	Vertical Suplex	Up, Tieup or Down, Tieup
7	Brainbuster	Left, Right, Kick or Right, Left, Kick
8	Power Bomb	Left, Down, Punch or Right, Down, Punch
9	Piledriver	Left, Up, Tieup or Right, Down, Tieup
9	Mandible Claw	Left, Right, Tieup or Right, Left, Tieup

Corner (Facing)

DAMAGE	NAME	MOVE
3	Kick in Corner	Kick
1	Forearm Smashes	Punch (Repeating)
1	Charging Shoulder	Tieup (Repeating)
5	Swinging DDT	Left, Left, Kick or Right, Right, Kick
5	Swinging DDT	Up, Up, Kick or Down, Down, Kick
7	Tree of Woe	Left, Left, Punch or Right, Right, Punch
7	Tree of Woe	Up, Up, Punch or Down, Down, Punch

Mankind

DAMAGE	NAME	MOVE
5	Top Rope Superplex	Left, Left, Tieup or Right, Right, Tieup
5	Top Rope Superplex	Up, Up, Tieup or Down, Down, Tieup

Corner (Behind)

DAMAGE	NAME	MOVE
1	Head into Turnbuckle	Kick (Repeating)
1	Head into Turnbuckle	Punch (Repeating)
1	Head into Turnbuckle	Tieup (Repeating)
5	Pump Handle Slam	Left, Tieup or Right Tieup
5	Pump Handle Slam	Up, Tieup or Down Tieup

Corner (Running)

DAMAGE	NAME	MOVE
3	Charging Clothesline	Kick
3	Charging Clothesline	Punch
3	Charging Clothesline	Tieup

Ready

DAMAGE	NAME	MOVE
5	Body Slam	Left, Up, Tieup or Right, Up, Tieup

DAMAGE	NAME	MOVE
5	Clothesline	Up, Up, Punch or Down, Down, Punch
5	Cobra Clutch	Up, Up, Tieup or Down, Down, Tieup
7	DDT	Left, Down, Kick or Right, Down, Kick
6	Front Backbreaker	Left, Right, Tieup or Right, Left, Tieup
6	Gut Wrench	Left, Right, Punch or Right, Left, Punch
3	Hiptoss	Up, Down, Kick or Down, Up, Kick
4	Kneebreaker	Left, Down, Tieup or Right, Down, Tieup
3	Leg Drag	Up, Up, Kick or Down, Down, Kick
9	Mandible Claw	Left, Right, Up, Tieup + Block or Right, Left, Up, Tieup + Block
5	Neck Breaker	Left, Down, Punch or Right, Down, Punch
6	Samoan Drop	Left, Up, Punch or Right, Up, Punch
6	Side Belly Belly Suplex	Up, Down, Tieup or Down, Up, Tieup
6	Single Arm DDT	Left, Up, Kick or Right, Up, Kick

Mankind

Ground Holds (At Feet)

DAMAGE	NAME	MOVE
5	Elbow Drop Onto Leg	Left, Left, Kick or Right, Right, Kick
5	Elbow Drop Onto Leg	Up, Up, Kick or Down, Down, Kick
6	Leg Grapevine	Left, Right, Kick or Right, Left, Kick
6	Headbutt to Groin	Up, Down, Kick or Down, Up, Kick
7	Reverse Indian Deathlock	Left, Right, Up, Kick or Right, Left, Down, Kick

Ground Holds (At Head)

DAMAGE	NAME	MOVE
5	Arm Wrench	Left, Left, Punch or Right, Right, Punch
5	Arm Wrench	Up, Up, Punch or Down, Down, Punch
6	Knee to Back	Left, Right, Punch or Right, Left, Punch
6	Painkiller	Up, Down, Punch or Down, Up, Punch
9	Mandible Claw	Right, Left, Up, Tieup + Block or Left, Right, Up, Tieup + Block

Ground Hits (Standing)

DAMAGE	NAME	MOVE
3	Leg Drop (at side)	Kick
1	Stomp	Kick
2	Elbow Drop	Punch
3	Knee Drop	Down, Kick

Ground Hits (Running)

DAMAGE	NAME	MOVE
3	Running Knee Drop	Kick
3	Fist Drop	Punch
4	Falling Headbutt	Tieup

Running Opponent

DAMAGE	NAME	MOVE
5	Flying Back Elbow	Kick
6	Back Body Drop	Punch
2	Arm Drag	Tieup
7	Power Slam	Up, Tieup or Down, Tieup

Kicks/Punches

DAMAGE	NAME	MOVE
2	Quick Kick	Kick
3	Kick	Left, Kick or Right, Kick
2	Punch	Punch
5	Haymaker	Up, Punch or Down, Punch
5	Haymaker	Left, Punch or Right, Punch

Running

DAMAGE	NAME	MOVE
5	Clothesline Running	Punch
5	Spinning Neck Breaker	Kick
5	Tackle with Punches	Tieup

Turnbuckle (Opponent On Ground)

DAMAGE	NAME	MOVE
6	Elbow Drop	Kick
6	Elbow Drop	Punch
6	Elbow Drop	Tieup

DAMAGE	NAME	MOVE
7	Splash	Punch + Tieup
7	Splash	Kick + Block
8	Somersault Senton Splash	Up, Up, Punch + Kick

Turnbuckle (Opponent Standing)

DAMAGE	NAME	MOVE
6	Axhandle Smash	Kick
6	Axhandle Smash	Punch
6	Axhandle Smash	Tieup
7	Bionic Elbow	Kick + Block
7	Clothesline Turnbuckle	Punch + Tieup
8	Forearm Smash	Up, Up, Tieup + Block

Apron (Opponent On Ground)

DAMAGE	NAME	MOVE
6	Elbow Drop	Kick
6	Elbow Drop	Punch
6	Elbow Drop	Tieup
7	Driving Elbow	Kick + Block
7	Splash	Punch + Tieup

Apron (Opponent Standing)

DAMAGE	NAME	MOVE
6	Axhandle Smash	Kick
6	Axhandle Smash	Punch
6	Axhandle Smash	Tieup
7	Bionic Elbow	Kick + Block
7	Clothesline Apron	Punch +Tieup

Bret "Hit-Man" Hart

If it weren't for his charisma, Bret would have a considerable time against his fellow WWF opponents. Still, he's got quite the goody bag that he's more than eager to share with his not-so-friendly foes. Bret's Side Back Breaker and Sharp Shooter

are sure to put a dent in an opponent's thoughts that this is going to be any easy match. Keep in mind, however, that he's not the strongest ox in the box, so avoid going toe-to-toe when you've met your match.

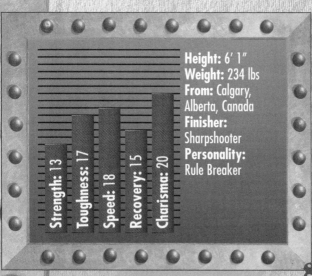

Height: 6' 1"
Weight: 234 lbs
From: Calgary, Alberta, Canada
Finisher: Sharpshooter
Personality: Rule Breaker

Strength: 13
Toughness: 17
Speed: 18
Recovery: 15
Charisma: 20

Behind Opponent

DAMAGE	NAME	MOVE
6	Cross Face Chicken Wing	Kick
6	Cross Face Chicken Wing	Punch
6	Cross Face Chicken Wing	Tieup
7	Russian Leg Sweep	Left, Left, Kick or Right, Right, Kick
7	Russian Leg Sweep	Up, Up, Kick or Down, Down, Kick
7	Atomic Drop	Left, Left, Punch or Right, Right, Punch
7	Atomic Drop	Up, Up, Punch or Down, Down, Punch
8	German Suplex	Left, Left, Up, Tieup or Right, Right, Up, Tieup

Tieup

DAMAGE	NAME	MOVE
1	Hiptoss	Kick
2	Top Wristlock	Punch
3	Atomic Drop	Tieup
4	Neck Breaker	Left, Kick or Right, Kick
4	Neck Breaker	Up, Kick or Down, Kick

DAMAGE	NAME	MOVE
5	Inverted Atomic Drop	Left, Punch or Right, Punch
5	Inverted Atomic Drop	Up, Punch or Down, Punch
6	Northern Lights Suplex	Left, Tieup or Right, Tieup
6	Northern Lights Suplex	Up, Tieup or Down, Tieup
7	Samoan Drop	Left, Right, Kick or Right, Left, Kick
8	Piledriver	Left, Up, Punch or Right, Down, Punch
9	Side Back Breaker	Left, Left, Tieup or Right, Right, Tieup

Corner (Facing)

DAMAGE	NAME	MOVE
1	Forearm Smashes	Kick (Repeating)
1	Forearm Smashes	Tieup (Repeating)
1	Climb and Pummel	Punch (Repeating)
5	Monkey Flip	Left, Left, Kick or Right, Right, Kick
5	Monkey Flip	Up, Up, Kick or Down, Down, Kick
5	Swinging DDT	Left, Left, Kick or Right, Right, Punch
5	Swinging DDT	Up, Up, Punch or Down, Down, Punch

Bret "Hit Man" Hart

91

DAMAGE	NAME	MOVE
5	Belly Belly Suplex	Left, Left, Kick or Right, Right, Tieup
5	Belly Belly Suplex	Up, Up, Kick or Down, Down, Tieup
7	Top Rope Superplex	Left, Right, Left, Kick or Right, Left, Right, Kick

Corner (Behind)

DAMAGE	NAME	MOVE
1	Head into Turnbuckle	Kick
1	Head into Turnbuckle	Punch
1	Head into Turnbuckle	Tieup
5	Pump Handle Slam	Left, Tieup or Right, Tieup
5	Pump Handle Slam	Up, Tieup or Down, Tieup

Corner (Running)

DAMAGE	NAME	MOVE
3	Charging Clothesline	Kick
3	Charging Clothesline	Punch
3	Charging Clothesline	Tieup

DAMAGE	NAME	MOVE
5	Body Slam	Left, Down, Tieup or Right, Down, Tieup
5	Clothesline	Left, Up, Kick or Right, Up, Kick
3	Crucifix	Left, Left, Kick or Right, Right, Kick
4	Fireman's Carry	Down, Down, Kick
3	Drop Toe Hold	Down, Down, Punch
3	Hiptoss	Up, Up, Kick
4	Kneebreaker	Right, Left, Tieup or Left, Right, Tieup
3	Leg Drag	Left, Down, Kick or Right, Down, Kick
6	Overhead Belly Belly Suplex	Left, Left, Punch or Right, Right, Punch
6	Samoan Drop	Left, Up, Punch or Right, Up, Punch
1	Small Package	Down, Down, Tieup
6	Spinebuster	Up, Down, Tieup or Down, Up, Tieup
7	Vertical Suplex	Up, Down, Punch or Down, Up, Punch

Bret "Hit Man" Hart

Ground Holds (At Feet)

DAMAGE	NAME	MOVE
5	Elbow Drop Onto Leg	Left, Left, Kick or Right, Right, Kick
5	Elbow Drop Onto Leg	Up, Up, Kick or Down, Down, Kick
6	Half Crab	Left, Right, Kick or Right, Left, Kick
6	Headbutt to Groin	Up, Down, Kick or Down, Up, Kick
9	Sharp Shooter	Right, Right, Up, Kick + Block or Left, Left, Up, Kick + Block

Ground Holds (At Head)

DAMAGE	NAME	MOVE
5	Leg Lock Chokehold	Left, Left, Punch or Right, Right, Punch
5	Leg Lock Chokehold	Up, Up, Punch or Down, Down, Punch
6	Rear Chin Lock	Left, Right, Punch or Right, Left, Punch
6	Short Arm Scissor	Up, Down, Punch or Down, Up, Punch
7	Painkiller	Left, Up, Down, Punch or Right, Down, Up, Punch

Ground Hits (Standing)

DAMAGE	NAME	MOVE
1	Stomp	Kick
3	Leg Drop (at side)	Kick
3	Knee Drop	Down, Kick
2	Fist Drop	Punch
1	Driving Elbow Smash	Down, Punch (Repeating Punch)

Ground Hits (Running)

DAMAGE	NAME	MOVE
3	Fist Drop	Kick
3	Fist Drop	Punch
4	Splash	Tieup

Running Opponent

DAMAGE	NAME	MOVE
5	Drop Kick	Kick
5	Flying Back Elbow	Punch
3	Drop Toe Hold	Tieup
7	Power Slam	Up, Tieup or Down, Tieup

Kicks/Punches

DAMAGE	NAME	MOVE
3	Kick	Kick
5	Drop Kick	Up, Kick
2	Punch	Punch
3	Inside Forearm	Left, Punch or Right, Punch
5	Haymaker	Up, Punch or Down, Punch

Running

DAMAGE	NAME	MOVE
5	Drop Kick Running	Kick
7	Hart Attack	Punch
5	Spinning Neck Breaker	Tieup
3	Crucifix	Punch + Tieup

Turnbuckle (Opponent On Ground)

DAMAGE	NAME	MOVE
6	Knee Drop	Kick
6	Knee Drop	Punch
6	Knee Drop	Tieup

DAMAGE	NAME	MOVE
7	Driving Elbow	Kick + Block
7	Elbow Drop	Punch + Tieup
8	Kamikaze Headbutt	Left, Right, Punch + Kick or Right, Left, Punch + Kick

Turnbuckle (Opponent Standing)

DAMAGE	NAME	MOVE
6	Drop Kick Turnbuckle	Kick
6	Drop Kick Turnbuckle	Punch
6	Drop Kick Turnbuckle	Tieup
7	Bionic Elbow	Kick + Block
3	Sunset Flip (in front of opponent)	Punch + Tieup
6	Drop Kick Turnbuckle	Punch + Tieup
8	Body Press (in front of opponent)	Up, Left, Tieup + Block or Up, Right, Tieup + Block

Apron (Opponent On Ground)

DAMAGE	NAME	MOVE
6	Knee Drop	Kick
6	Knee Drop	Punch
6	Knee Drop	Tieup
7	Driving Elbow	Kick + Block
7	Elbow Drop	Punch + Tieup

Apron (Opponent Standing)

DAMAGE	NAME	MOVE
6	Drop Kick Apron	Kick
6	Drop Kick Apron	Punch
6	Drop Kick Apron	Tieup
7	Bionic Elbow	Kick + Block
7	Clothesline Apron	Punch + Tieup

Owen Hart

Owen's about as fast as they come, and unlike many of the other wrestlers in the game, he actually has four moves that are rated a 9 when it comes to damage. His Double Underhook Suplex, the Sharpshooter, the Shooting Star Press, and the Wheel Kick can cause plenty of damage. But like Bret, Owen isn't the strongest of wrestlers, so keep your guard up!

Strength: 13
Toughness: 17
Speed: 22
Recovery: 17
Charisma: 15

Height: 5' 11"
Weight: 227 lbs
From: Calgary, Alberta, Canada
Finisher: Sharpshooter
Personality: Rule Breaker

Behind Opponent

DAMAGE	NAME	MOVE
6	Cross Face Chicken Wing	Kick
6	Cross Face Chicken Wing	Punch
6	Cross Face Chicken Wing	Tieup
7	Atomic Drop	Left, Left, Kick or Right, Right, Kick
7	Atomic Drop	Up, Up, Kick or Down, Down, Kick
7	Belly Back Suplex	Left, Left, Punch or Right, Right, Punch
7	Belly Back Suplex	Up, Up, Punch or Down, Down, Punch
3	Victory Roll	Left, Left, Tieup or Right, Right, Tieup
3	Victory Roll	Up, Up, Tieup or Down, Down, Tieup
8	German Suplex	Left, Left, Up, Tieup or Right, Right, Up, Tieup

Tieup

DAMAGE	NAME	MOVE
1	Arm Drag	Kick
2	Neck Breaker	Punch
3	Side Belly Belly Suplex	Tieup

Chapter 8

DAMAGE	NAME	MOVE
4	Gut Wrench Power Bomb	Left, Kick or Right, Kick
4	Gut Wrench Power Bomb	Up, Kick or Down, Kick
5	Samoan Drop	Left, Punch or Right, Punch
5	Samoan Drop	Up, Punch or Down, Punch
6	Vertical Suplex	Left, Tieup or Right, Tieup
6	Vertical Suplex	Up, Tieup or Down, Tieup
7	Overhead Belly Belly Suplex	Left, Up, Kick or Right, Down, Kick
8	Piledriver	Up, Down, Punch or Down, Up, Punch
9	Double Underhook Suplex	Up, Down, Tieup or Down, Up, Tieup

Corner (Facing)

DAMAGE	NAME	MOVE
3	Kick to Ribs	Kick
1	Climb and Pummel	Punch (Repeating)
3	Splash in Corner	Tieup
5	Flying Head Scissors	Left, Left, Kick or Right, Right, Kick
5	Flying Head Scissors	Up, Up, Kick or Down, Down, Kick

DAMAGE	NAME	MOVE
5	Monkey Flip	Left, Left, Punch or Right, Right, Punch
5	Monkey Flip	Up, Up, Punch or Down, Down, Punch
5	Swinging DDT	Left, Left, Tieup or Right, Right, Tieup
5	Swinging DDT	Up, Up, Tieup or Down, Down, Tieup
7	Hurricanranna	Left, Right, Up, Kick or Right, Left, Up, Kick
8	Superplex	Up, Right, Down, Punch or Down, Left, Up, Punch

Corner (Behind)

DAMAGE	NAME	MOVE
1	Head into Turnbuckle	Kick (Repeating)
1	Head into Turnbuckle	Punch (Repeating)
1	Head into Turnbuckle	Tieup (Repeating)
5	Pump Handle Slam	Left, Tieup or Right, Tieup
5	Pump Handle Slam	Up, Tieup or Down, Tieup

Corner (Running)

DAMAGE	NAME	MOVE
3	Avalanche	Kick
3	Avalanche	Punch
3	Avalanche	Tieup

Ready

DAMAGE	NAME	MOVE
4	Abdominal Stretch	Left, Down, Punch or Right, Down, Punch
2	Arm Drag	Up, Up, Punch
6	Overhead Belly Belly Suplex	Left, Left, Tieup or Right, Right, Tieup
7	Double Underhook Suplex	Down, Down, Tieup
5	Flying Head Scissors	Left, Left, Kick or Right, Right, Kick
3	Drop Toe Hold	Down, Down, Kick
8	Hurricanranna	Left, Right, Up, Kick or Right, Left, Up, Kick
6	Gut Wrench	Left, Right, Punch or Right, Left, Punch
2	Japanese Arm Drag	Down, Down, Punch
6	Fisherman's Suplex	Up, Up, Tieup

DAMAGE	NAME	MOVE
6	Side Belly Belly Suplex	Left, Up, Punch or Right, Up, Punch
2	Small Package	Left, Up, Tieup or Right, Up, Tieup
5	Snap Mare	Left, Down, Kick or Right, Down, Kick

Ground Holds (At Feet)

DAMAGE	NAME	MOVE
5	Surfboard	Left, Left, Kick or Right, Right, Kick
5	Surfboard	Up, Up, Kick or Down, Down, Kick
6	Leg Grapevine	Left, Right, Kick or Right, Left, Kick
6	Wishbone Leg Splitter	Up, Down, Kick or Down, Up, Kick
7	Reverse Indian Deathlock	Left, Right, Up, Kick or Right, Left, Down, Kick
8	Inverted STF	Up, Left, Up, Kick or Down, Right, Down, Kick
9	Sharp Shooter	Left, Left, Up, Kick + Block or Right, Right, Up, Kick + Block

Ground Holds (At Head)

DAMAGE	NAME	MOVE
5	Arm Wrench	Left, Left, Punch or Right, Right, Punch
5	Arm Wrench	Up, Up, Punch or Down, Down, Punch
6	Rear Chin Lock	Left, Right, Punch or Right, Left, Punch
6	Leg Lock Choke Hold	Up, Down, Punch or Down, Up, Punch

Ground Hits (Standing)

DAMAGE	NAME	MOVE
1	Stomp	Kick
3	Falling Headbutt	Down, Kick
2	Elbow Drop	Punch
4	Splash Down	Punch

Ground Hits (Running)

DAMAGE	NAME	MOVE
3	Running Knee Drop	Kick
3	Fist Drop	Punch
4	Falling Headbutt	Tieup

Owen Hart

Running Opponent

DAMAGE	NAME	MOVE
5	Drop Kick	Kick
6	Back Body Drop	Punch
7	Running Belly Belly Plex	Tieup
8	Hurricanranna	Up, Kick or Down, Kick

Kicks/Punches

DAMAGE	NAME	MOVE
3	Kick	Kick
5	Drop Kick	Up, Kick or Down, Kick
2	Grab and Punch	Punch
3	Inside Forearm	Up, Punch or Down, Punch
2	Punch	Left, Punch or Right, Punch

Running

DAMAGE	NAME	MOVE
6	Spinning Heel Kick	Kick
5	Flying Clothesline	Punch
4	Flying Forearm	Tieup

DAMAGE	NAME	MOVE
8	Hurricanranna	Kick + Block

Turnbuckle (Opponent On Ground)

DAMAGE	NAME	MOVE
6	Kamikaze Headbutt	Kick
6	Kamikaze Headbutt	Punch
6	Kamikaze Headbutt	Tieup
7	Somersault Senton Splash	Kick + Block
7	Splash	Punch + Tieup
9	Shooting Star Press	Up, Up, Kick + Tieup
5	Moonsault (at side)	Block

Turnbuckle (Opponent Standing)

DAMAGE	NAME	MOVE
6	Forearm Smash	Kick
6	Forearm Smash	Punch
6	Forearm Smash	Tieup
7	Hurricanranna	Kick + Block

DAMAGE	NAME	MOVE
7	Torpedo Dropkick	Punch + Tieup
9	Wheel Kick	Left, Left, Kick + Tieup or Right, Right, Kick + Tieup
3	Sunset Flip	Punch + Kick + Tieup

Apron (Opponent On Ground)

DAMAGE	NAME	MOVE
6	Kamikaze Headbutt	Kick
6	Kamikaze Headbutt	Punch
6	Kamikaze Headbutt	Tieup
7	Somersault Senton Splash	Kick + Block
7	Splash	Punch + Tieup

Apron (Opponent Standing)

DAMAGE	NAME	MOVE
6	Forearm Smash	Kick
6	Forearm Smash	Punch
6	Forearm Smash	Tieup
7	Hurricanranna	Kick + Block
7	Torpedo DropKick	Punch + Tieup

The Undertaker

The Undertaker's a monster at 6' 10" and his strength and toughness (as well as his slow speed) prove that point. Surprisingly, he has only two 9 point damage moves: the Choke Slam and the Tombstone Piledriver. He does, however, have lots

of mid-range moves to round out his arsenal. Still, considering his recovery rating on top of everything else, The Undertaker is sure to send more than a few wrestlers to an early grave.

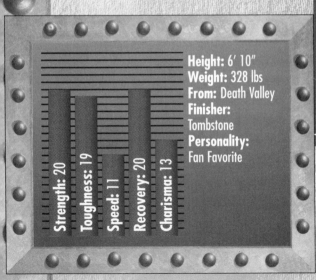

Strength: 20
Toughness: 19
Speed: 11
Recovery: 20
Charisma: 13

Height: 6' 10"
Weight: 328 lbs
From: Death Valley
Finisher: Tombstone
Personality: Fan Favorite

The Undertaker

Behind Opponent

DAMAGE	NAME	MOVE
6	Neck Breaker	Kick
6	Neck Breaker	Punch
6	Neck Breaker	Tieup
7	Reverse DDT	Left, Left, Kick or Right, Right, Kick
7	Reverse DDT	Up, Up, Kick or Down, Down, Kick
7	Reverse DDT	Left, Left, Punch or Right, Right, Punch
7	Reverse DDT	Up, Up, Punch or Down, Down, Punch
8	Side Slam	Left, Left, Up, Tieup or Right, Right, Up, Tieup

Tieup

DAMAGE	NAME	MOVE
1	Back Breaker	Kick
2	Atomic Drop	Punch
3	Sidewalk Slam	Tieup
4	Northern Lights Suplex	Left, Kick or Right, Kick
4	Northern Lights Suplex	Up, Kick or Down, Kick
5	DDT	Left, Punch or Right, Punch

DAMAGE	NAME	MOVE
5	DDT	Up, Punch or Down, Punch
6	Gut Wrench Power Bomb	Left, Tieup or Right, Tieup
6	Gut Wrench Power Bomb	Up, Tieup or Down, Tieup
7	Vertical Suplex	Left, Down, Kick or Right, Down, Kick
8	Overhead Belly Belly Suplex	Left, Up, Punch or Right, Up, Punch
9	Choke Slam	Left, Right, Tieup or Right, Left, Tieup
9	Tombstone Piledrive	Up, Down, Tieup or Down, Up, Tieup

Corner (Facing)

DAMAGE	NAME	MOVE
3	Choke with Boot	Kick
1	Climb and Pummel	Punch (Repeating)
3	Choke with Boot	Tieup
5	Overhead Press	Left, Left, Kick or Right, Right, Kick
5	Overhead Press	Up, Up, Kick or Down, Down, Kick
5	Belly Belly Suplex	Left, Left, Punch or Right, Right, Punch
5	Belly Belly Suplex	Up, Up, Punch or Down, Down, Punch

DAMAGE	NAME	MOVE
5	Top Rope Double Underhook	Left, Left, Tieup or Right, Right, Tieup
5	Top Rope Double Underhook	Up, Up, Tieup or Down, Down, Tieup
7	Top Rope Superplex	Up, Up, Down, Kick or Down, Down, Up, Kick

Corner (Behind)

DAMAGE	NAME	MOVE
1	Head into Turnbuckle	Kick (Repeating)
1	Head into Turnbuckle	Punch (Repeating)
1	Head into Turnbuckle	Tieup (Repeating)
5	Pump Handle Slam	Left, Tieup or Right, Tieup
5	Pump Handle Slam	Up, Tieup or Down, Tieup

Corner (Running)

DAMAGE	NAME	MOVE
3	Charging Clothesline	Kick
3	Charging Clothesline	Punch
3	Charging Clothesline	Tieup

Ready

DAMAGE	NAME	MOVE
6	Front Face DDT	Left, Left, Tieup or Right, Right, Tieup
6	Overhead Belly Belly Suplex	Left, Down, Tieup or Right, Down, Tieup
6	Choke Slam	Down, Down, Punch
7	DDT	Left, Down, Kick or Right, Down, Kick
6	Gut Wrench	Left, Right, Punch or Right, Left, Punch
5	Neck Breaker	Left, Down, Punch or Right, Down, Punch
6	Side Belly Belly Suplex	Right, Left, Tieup or Left, Right, Tieup
5	Short Arm Clothesline	Left, Up, Tieup or Right, Up, Tieup
6	Single Arm DDT	Left, Up, Kick or Right, Up, Kick
5	Snap Mare	Left, Up, Punch or Right, Up, Punch
6	Throat Toss	Down, Up, Tieup
9	Tombstone Piledriver	Down, Down, Down, Punch + Tieup
7	Vertical Suplex	Left, Right, Kick or Right, Left, Kick

Ground Holds (At Feet)

DAMAGE	NAME	MOVE
5	Elbow Drop Onto Leg	Left, Left, Kick or Right, Right, Kick
5	Elbow Drop Onto Leg	Up, Up, Kick or Down, Down, Kick
6	Half Crab	Left, Right, Kick or Right, Left, Kick
6	Surfboard	Up, Down, Kick or Down, Up, Kick
7	Leg Lock	Left, Right, Left, Kick or Right, Left, Right, Kick

Ground Holds (At Head)

DAMAGE	NAME	MOVE
5	Arm Wrench	Left, Left, Punch or Right, Right, Punch
5	Arm Wrench	Up, Up, Punch or Down, Down, Punch
6	Squeeze Head	Left, Right, Punch or Right, Left, Punch
6	Painkiller	Up, Down, Punch or Down, Up, Punch

Ground Hits (Standing)

DAMAGE	NAME	MOVE
3	Leg Drop (at side)	Kick
1	Stomp	Kick
3	Knee Drop	Down, Kick
2	Elbow Drop	Punch

Ground Hits (Running)

DAMAGE	NAME	MOVE
4	Leg Drop (at side)	Kick
3	Fist Drop	Kick
3	Fist Drop	Punch
4	Falling Headbutt	Tieup

Running Opponent

DAMAGE	NAME	MOVE
4	Boot to Face	Kick
5	Clothesline	Punch
7	Powerslam	Tieup
8	Spinebuster	Left, Tieup or Right, Tieup

Kicks/Punches

DAMAGE	NAME	MOVE
2	Quick Kick	Kick
3	Kick	Left, Kick or Right, Kick
6	Thrust to Throat	Punch
3	Choke	Up, Punch or Down, Punch
5	Haymaker	Left, Punch or Right, Punch

Running

DAMAGE	NAME	MOVE
5	Flying Clothesline	Punch
5	Flying Clothesline	Kick
5	Spinning Neck Breaker	Tieup

Turnbuckle (Opponent On Ground)

DAMAGE	NAME	MOVE
6	Fist Drop	Kick
6	Fist Drop	Punch
6	Fist Drop	Tieup

DAMAGE	NAME	MOVE
7	Double Foot Stomp	Kick + Block
7	Splash	Punch + Tieup
8	Driving Elbow	Left, Right, Kick + Tieup, Right, Left, Kick + Tieup

Turnbuckle (Opponent Standing)

DAMAGE	NAME	MOVE
6	Drop Kick Turnbuckle	Kick
6	Drop Kick Turnbuckle	Punch
6	Drop Kick Turnbuckle	Tieup
7	Axhandle Smash	Kick + Block
7	Clothesline Turnbuckle	Punch + Tieup
8	Forearm Smash	Left, Right, Kick + Tieup or Right, Left, Kick + Tieup

Apron (Opponent On Ground)

DAMAGE	NAME	MOVE
6	Fist Drop	Kick
6	Fist Drop	Punch
6	Fist Drop	Tieup
7	Double Foot Stomp	Kick + Block
7	Splash	Punch + Tieup

Apron (Opponent Standing)

DAMAGE	NAME	MOVE
6	Drop Kick Apron	Kick
6	Drop Kick Apron	Punch
6	Drop Kick Apron	Tieup
7	Axhandle Smash	Kick + Block
7	Clothesline Apron	Punch + Tieup

Ken Shamrock

For the quick (and Shamrock is nothing, if not quick), Ken can provide plenty of hurt with his Shamrock Ankle Lock and his Side Belly Belly Suplex. Although he's a relatively average wrestler, he has quite the assortment of moves to help make up for less than perfect stats. Ken possesses such moves as the Fuji Arm Bar and the Hurricanranna. Relying on his ratings alone can be deceiving, because Ken can go mano-a-mano with the best of 'em!

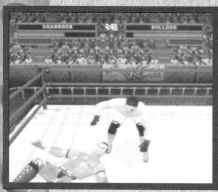

Height: 6' 1"
Weight: 245 lbs
From: Sacremento, CA
Finisher: Ankle Lock Submission
Personality: Fan Favorite

Strength: 17
Toughness: 17
Speed: 20
Recovery: 15
Charisma: 15

Behind Opponent

DAMAGE	NAME	MOVE
6	Russian Leg Sweep	Kick
6	Russian Leg Sweep	Punch
6	Russian Leg Sweep	Tieup
7	Pump Handle Slam	Left, Left, Kick or Right, Right, Kick
7	Pump Handle Slam	Up, Up, Kick or Down, Down, Kick
7	Reverse DDT	Left, Left, Punch or Right, Right, Punch
7	Reverse DDT	Up, Up, Punch or Down, Down, Punch
3	Victory Roll	Left, Left, Tieup or Right, Right, Tieup
3	Victory Roll	Up, Down, Tieup or Down, Up, Tieup
8	Belly Back Suplex	Left, Up, Right, Tieup or Right, Up, Left, Tieup

Tieup

DAMAGE	NAME	MOVE
1	Hiptoss	Kick
2	Top Wristlock	Punch
3	Sidewalk Slam	Tieup

DAMAGE	NAME	MOVE
4	Northern Lights Suplex	Left, Kick or Right, Kick
4	Northern Lights Suplex	Up, Kick or Down, Kick
5	Gut Wrench Power Bomb	Left, Punch or Right, Punch
5	Gut Wrench Power Bomb	Up, Punch or Down, Punch
6	Vertical Suplex	Left, Tieup or Right, Tieup
6	Vertical Suplex	Up, Tieup or Down, Tieup
7	Overhead Belly Belly Suplex	Left, Up, Kick or Right, Up, Kick
8	Double Underhook Suplex	Left, Right, Punch or Right, Left, Punch
9	Side Belly Belly Suplex	Left, Down, Tieup or Right, Down, Tieup

Corner (Facing)

DAMAGE	NAME	MOVE
1	Chest Chop	Kick (Repeating)
1	Climb and Pummel	Punch (Repeating)
1	Charging Shoulder	Tieup (Repeating)
5	Flying Head Scissors	Left, Left, Kick or Right, Right, Kick
5	Flying Head Scissors	Up, Up, Kick or Down, Down, Kick

DAMAGE	NAME	MOVE
5	Hurricanranna	Left, Left, Punch or Right, Right, Punch
5	Hurricanranna	Up, Down, Punch or Down, Up, Punch
5	Superplex	Left, Left, Tieup or Right, Right, Tieup
5	Superplex	Up, Down, Tieup or Down, Up, Tieup
7	Top Rope Superplex	Up, Down, Up, Tieup or Down, Up, Down, Tieup

Corner (Behind)

DAMAGE	NAME	MOVE
1	Head into Turnbuckle	Kick (Repeating)
1	Head into Turnbuckle	Punch (Repeating)
1	Head into Turnbuckle	Tieup (Repeating)
5	Pump Handle Slam	Left, Tieup or Right, Tieup
5	Pump Handle Slam	Up, Tieup or Down, Tieup

Corner (Running)

DAMAGE	NAME	MOVE
3	Avalanche	Kick
3	Avalanche	Punch
3	Avalanche	Tieup

DAMAGE	NAME	MOVE
6	Front Face DDT	Left, Right, Punch or Right, Left, Punch
2	Arm Wrench	Left, Left, Punch or Right, Right, Punch
3	Crucifix	Left, Right, Kick or Right, Left, Kick
8	Hurricanranna	Left, Right, Up, Kick or Right, Left, Up, Kick
2	Japanese Arm Drag	Down, Down, Punch
4	Kneebreaker	Left, Down, Kick or Right, Down, Kick
3	Leg Drag	Left, Left, Kick or Right, Right, Kick
5	Reverse Pain Killer	Left, Down, Punch or Right, Down, Punch
6	Samoan Drop	Left, Up, Punch or Right, Up, Punch
5	Short Arm Clothesline	Up, Up, Punch
7	Sidewalk Slam	Left, Down, Tieup or Right, Down, Tieup
6	Single Arm DDT	Left, Up, Kick or Right, Up, Kick
1	Small Package	Up, Down, Tieup or Down, Up, Tieup

Ken Shamrock

DAMAGE	NAME	MOVE
5	Spinning Neck Breaker	Left, Left, Tieup or Right, Right, Tieup

Ground Holds (At Feet)

DAMAGE	NAME	MOVE
5	Leg Grapevine	Left, Left, Kick or Right, Right, Kick
5	Leg Grapevine	Up, Up, Kick or Down, Down, Kick
6	Texas Cloverleaf	Left, Right, Kick or Right, Left, Kick
6	STF	Up, Down, Kick or Down, Up, Kick
7	Inverted STF	Up, Left, Up, Kick or Down, Right, Down, Kick
8	Reverse Fuji Leg Bar	Left, Up, Right, Kick or Right, Up, Left, Kick
9	Shamrock Ankle Lock	Left, Right, Up, Kick + Tieup or Right, Left, Up, Kick + Tieup

Ground Holds (At Head)

DAMAGE	NAME	MOVE
5	Leg Lock Chokehold	Left, Left, Punch or Right, Right, Punch

Chapter 8

DAMAGE	NAME	MOVE
5	Leg Lock Chokehold	Up, Up, Punch or Down, Down, Punch
6	Reverse Chinlock	Left, Right, Punch or Right, Left, Punch
6	Short Arm Scissor	Up, Down, Punch or Down, Up, Punch
7	Painkiller	Left, Up, Down, Punch or Right, Down, Up, Punch
8	Fuji Arm Bar	Up, Left, Up, Punch or Down, Right, Down, Punch

Ground Hits (Standing)

DAMAGE	NAME	MOVE
1	Stomp	Kick
3	Falling Headbutt	Down, Kick
2	Elbow Drop	Punch
4	Standing Moonsault (at side)	Down, Punch
1	Driving Elbow Smash	Down, Punch (Repeating Punch)

Ken Shamrock

Ground Hits (Running)

DAMAGE	NAME	MOVE
3	Fist Drop	Kick
3	Front Elbow	Punch
3	Fist Drop	Tieup

Running Opponent

DAMAGE	NAME	MOVE
3	Drop Toe Hold	Kick
5	Clothesline	Punch
7	Running Belly Belly Plex	Tieup
8	Hurricanranna	Up, Kick or Down, Kick

Kicks/Punches

DAMAGE	NAME	MOVE
1	Kick to Thighs	Kick
2	Quick Kick	Kick
5	Drop Kick	Up, Kick
3	Grab and Punch	Punch
3	Discus Punch	Up, Punch or Down, Punch
2	Forearm	Left, Punch or Right, Punch

Running

DAMAGE	NAME	MOVE
5	Tackle with Punches	Kick
5	Clothesline Running	Punch
5	Cross Body Block	Tieup
8	Hurricanranna	Punch + Tieup

Turnbuckle (Opponent On Ground)

DAMAGE	NAME	MOVE
6	Elbow Drop	Kick
6	Elbow Drop	Punch
6	Elbow Drop	Tieup
7	Double Foot Stomp	Kick + Block
7	Kamikaze Headbutt	Punch + Tieup
8	Splash	Left, Left, Punch + Kick or Right, Right, Punch + Kick
5	Moonsault	Block

Ken Shamrock

Turnbuckle (Opponent Standing)

DAMAGE	NAME	MOVE
6	Drop Kick Turnbuckle	Kick
6	Drop Kick Turnbuckle	Punch
6	Drop Kick Turnbuckle	Tieup
7	Body Press	Kick + Block
7	Shoulder Tackle	Punch + Tieup
8	Hurricanranna	Left, Up, Kick + Tieup or Right, Up, Kick + Tieup

Apron (Opponent On Ground)

DAMAGE	NAME	MOVE
6	Elbow Drop	Kick
6	Elbow Drop	Punch
6	Elbow Drop	Tieup
7	Double Foot Stomp	Kick + Block
7	Kamikaze Headbutt	Punch + Tieup

Apron (Opponent Standing)

DAMAGE	NAME	MOVE
6	Drop Kick Apron	Kick
6	Drop Kick Apron	Punch
6	Drop Kick Apron	Tieup
7	Body Press	Kick + Block
7	Shoulder Tackle	Punch + Tieup

Ken Shamrock

Shawn Michaels

You thought Shamrock was fast? Well, you ain't seen nothing until you've taken a look at Shawn Michaels. Unfortunately, all that speed is needed to keep his opponent's solid blows from sending him to the ER. Although he does have a few killer moves (such as the Sweet Chin Music and the Piledriver), only the most experienced of players can make Michaels the champion he's set on becoming.

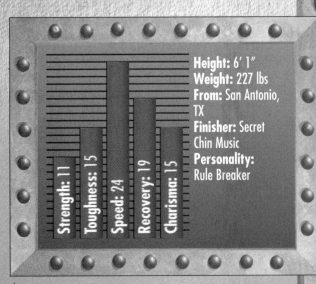

Strength: 11
Toughness: 15
Speed: 24
Recovery: 19
Charisma: 15

Height: 6' 1"
Weight: 227 lbs
From: San Antonio, TX
Finisher: Secret Chin Music
Personality: Rule Breaker

Behind Opponent

DAMAGE	NAME	MOVE
6	Abdominal Stretch	Kick
6	Abdominal Stretch	Punch
6	Abdominal Stretch	Tieup
7	Pump Handle Slam	Left, Left, Kick or Right, Right, Kick
7	Pump Handle Slam	Up, Up, Kick or Down, Down, Kick
3	Victory Roll	Left, Left, Punch or Right, Right, Punch
3	Victory Roll	Up, Up, Punch or Down, Down, Punch
8	German Suplex	Left, Left, Up, Tieup or Right, Right, Up, Tieup

Tieup

DAMAGE	NAME	MOVE
1	Arm Drag	Kick
2	Side Belly Belly Suplex	Punch
3	DDT	Tieup
4	Northern Lights Suplex	Left, Kick or Right, Kick

Shawn Michaels

DAMAGE	NAME	MOVE
4	Northern Lights Suplex	Up, Kick or Down, Kick
5	Samoan Drop	Left, Punch or Right, Punch
5	Samoan Drop	Up, Punch or Down, Punch
6	Overhead Belly Belly Suplex	Left, Tieup or Right, Tieup
6	Overhead Belly Belly Suplex	Up, Tieup or Down, Tieup
7	Double Underhook Suplex	Left, Right, Kick or Right, Left, Kick
8	Brainbuster	Up, Down, Punch or Down, Up, Punch
9	Piledriver	Left, Up, Tieup or Right, Down, Tieup

Corner (Facing)

DAMAGE	NAME	MOVE
1	Chest Chop	Kick (Repeating)
1	Climb and Pummel	Punch (Repeating)
3	Splash in Corner	Tieup
5	Flying Head Scissors	Left, Left, Kick or Right, Right, Kick

DAMAGE	NAME	MOVE
5	Flying Head Scissors	Up, Up, Kick or Down, Down, Kick
5	Monkey Flip	Left, Left, Punch or Right, Right, Punch
5	Monkey Flip	Up, Up, Punch or Down, Down, Punch
5	Swinging DDT	Left, Left, Tieup or Right, Right, Tieup
5	Swinging DDT	Up, Down, Tieup or Down, Up, Tieup
7	Hurricanranna	Left, Right, Up, Kick or Right, Left, Up, Kick
8	Top Rope Superplex	Up, Down, Up, Tieup or Down, Up, Down, Tieup

Corner (Behind)

DAMAGE	NAME	MOVE
1	Head into Turnbuckle	Kick (Repeating)
1	Head into Turnbuckle	Punch (Repeating)
1	Head into Turnbuckle	Tieup (Repeating)
5	Pump Handle Slam	Left, Tieup or Right, Tieup
5	Pump Handle Slam	Up, Tieup or Down, Tieup

Shawn Michaels

Corner (Running)

DAMAGE	NAME	MOVE
3	Avalanche	Kick
3	Avalanche	Punch
3	Avalanche	Tieup

Ready

DAMAGE	NAME	MOVE
2	Arm Drag	Up, Up, Punch
2	Arm Wrench	Left, Left, Punch or Right, Right, Punch
6	Overhead Belly Belly Suplex	Left, Right, Punch or Right, Left, Punch
5	Body Slam	Left, Down, Punch or Right, Down, Punch
3	Crucifix	Left, Left, Kick or Right, Right, Kick
7	DDT	Left, Down, Kick or Right, Down, Kick
5	Flying Head Scissors	Up, Up, Kick
3	Drop Toe Hold	Down, Down, Kick
8	Hurricanranna	Left, Right, Up, Kick or Right, Left, Up, Kick
3	Headlock Takedown	Left, Down, Tieup or Right, Down, Tieup

DAMAGE	NAME	MOVE
2	Japanese Arm Drag	Down, Down, Punch
6	Side Belly Belly Suplex	Left, Up, Tieup or Right, Up, Tieup
6	Single Arm DDT	Left, Up, Kick or Right, Up, Kick
1	Small Package	Down, Down, Tieup

Ground Holds (At Feet)

DAMAGE	NAME	MOVE
5	Knee to Inside Leg	Left, Left, Kick or Right, Right, Kick
5	Knee to Inside Leg	Up, Up, Kick or Down, Down, Kick
6	Step Over Toe Hold	Left, Right, Kick or Right, Left, Kick
6	Elbow to Groin	Up, Down, Kick or Down, Up, Kick
7	Figure Four Leglock	Left, Up, Left, Kick or Right, Down, Right, Kick

Ground Holds (At Head)

DAMAGE	NAME	MOVE
5	Arm Wrench	Left, Left, Punch or Right, Right, Punch
5	Arm Wrench	Up, Up, Punch or Down, Down, Punch

Shawn Michaels

DAMAGE	NAME	MOVE
6	Reverse Chin Lock	Left, Right, Punch or Right, Left, Punch
6	Leg Lock Chokehold	Up, Down, Punch or Down, Up, Punch

Ground Hits (Standing)

DAMAGE	NAME	MOVE
2	Elbow Drop	Punch
4	Standing Moonsault	Down, Punch
1	Stomp	Kick
3	Knee Drop	Down, Kick

Ground Hits (Running)

DAMAGE	NAME	MOVE
4	Leg Drop (at side)	Kick
3	Running Elbow Drop	Kick
3	Running Elbow Drop	Punch
3	Running Elbow Drop	Tieup

Running Opponent

DAMAGE	NAME	MOVE
5	Drop Kick	Kick
5	Back Body Drop	Punch

DAMAGE	NAME	MOVE
2	Arm Drag	Tieup
8	Hurricanranna	Up, Kick or Down, Kick

Kicks/Punches

DAMAGE	NAME	MOVE
3	Kick	Kick
5	Drop Kick	Up, Kick
2	Grab and Punch	Punch
3	Discus Punch	Up, Punch or Down, Punch
2	Inside Forearm	Left, Punch or Right, Punch
9	Sweet Chin Music	Left, Down, Up, Kick + Block or Right, Down, Up, Kick + Block

Running

DAMAGE	NAME	MOVE
5	Cross Body Block	Kick
5	Flying Clothesline	Punch
3	Crucifix	Tieup
8	Hurricanranna	Punch + Tieup

Shawn Michaels

Turnbuckle (Opponent On Ground)

DAMAGE	NAME	MOVE
6	Elbow Drop	Kick
6	Elbow Drop	Punch
6	Elbow Drop	Tieup
7	Fist Drop	Kick + Block
7	Splash	Punch + Tieup
8	Shooting Star Press	Up, Up, Kick + Tieup
5	Moonsault	Block (at side, opponent in ring)

Turnbuckle (Opponent Standing)

DAMAGE	NAME	MOVE
6	Drop Kick Turnbuckle	Kick
6	Drop Kick Turnbuckle	Punch
6	Drop Kick Turnbuckle	Tieup
7	Bionic Elbow	Punch + Tieup
3	Sunset Flip (opponent in ring)	Kick + Block

Chapter 8

DAMAGE	NAME	MOVE
7	Drop Kick Turnbuckle	Kick + Block
8	Hurricanranna	Left, Up, Kick + Tieup or Right, Up, Kick + Tieup
5	Moonsaul (opponent in ring)	Block

Apron (Opponent On Ground)

DAMAGE	NAME	MOVE
6	Elbow Drop	Kick
6	Elbow Drop	Punch
6	Elbow Drop	Tieup
7	Fist Drop	Kick + Block
7	Splash	Punch + Tieup

Apron (Opponent Standing)

DAMAGE	NAME	MOVE
6	Drop Kick Apron	Kick
6	Drop Kick Apron	Punch
6	Drop Kick Apron	Tieup
7	Bionic Elbow	Punch + Tieup
7	Bionic Elbow	Kick + Block

Shawn Michaels

Headbanger-Mosh

The Headbangers are quite the terrible two-some. However, when separated they aren't quite so fearsome, especially Mosh. Although his recovery is good and he can stir up the crowd, it's  going to take all the manual dexterity you can muster to master Mosh. He has a solid Power Bomb and opponents will want to steer clear of his Mosh Pit; however, the most experienced foe can easily make mush out of Mosh.

Strength: 15
Toughness: 17
Speed: 13
Recovery: 20
Charisma: 17

Height: 6' 0"
Weight: 243 lbs
From: His own private hell
Finisher: Mosh Pit
Personality: Fan Favorite

Behind Opponent

DAMAGE	NAME	MOVE
6	Neck Breaker	Kick
6	Neck Breaker	Punch
6	Neck Breaker	Tieup
7	Pump Handle Slam	Left, Left, Kick or Right, Right, Kick
7	Pump Handle Slam	Up, Up, Kick or Down, Down, Kick
7	Reverse DDT	Left, Left, Punch or Right, Right, Punch
7	Reverse DDT	Up, Up, Punch or Down, Down, Punch
3	Victory Roll	Left, Left, Tieup or Right, Right, Tieup
3	Victory Roll	Up, Up, Tieup or Down, Down, Tieup
8	German Suplex	Left, Left, Up, Tieup or Right, Right, Up, Tieup

Tieup

DAMAGE	NAME	MOVE
1	Hiptoss	Kick
2	Neck Breaker	Punch
3	Gut Wrench Power Bomb	Tieup
4	Sidewalk Slam	Left, Kick or Right, Kick
4	Sidewalk Slam	Up, Kick or Down, Kick

DAMAGE	NAME	MOVE
5	Samoan Drop	Left, Punch or Right, Punch
5	Samoan Drop	Up, Punch or Down, Punch
6	Vertical Suplex	Left, Tieup or Right, Tieup
6	Vertical Suplex	Up, Tieup or Down, Tieup
7	Brainbuster	Left, Up, Kick or Right, Up, Kick
8	Double Underhook Suplex	Left, Right, Punch or Right, Left, Punch
9	Power Bomb	Left, Down, Tieup or Right, Down, Tieup

Corner (Facing)

DAMAGE	NAME	MOVE
1	Chest Chop	Kick (Repeating)
1	Chest Chop	Punch (Repeating)
3	Splash in Corner	Tieup
5	Monkey Flip	Left, Left, Kick or Right, Right, Kick
5	Monkey Flip	Up, Up, Kick or Down, Down, Kick
5	Belly Belly Suplex	Left, Left, Punch or Right, Right, Punch
5	Belly Belly Suplex	Up, Up, Punch or Down, Down, Punch

DAMAGE	NAME	MOVE
5	Top Rope Superplex	Left, Left, Tieup or Right, Right, Tieup
5	Top Rope Superplex	Up, Down, Tieup or Down, Up, Tieup
7	Hurricanranna	Left, Right, Down, Kick or Right, Left, Down, Kick

Corner (Behind)

DAMAGE	NAME	MOVE
1	Head into Turnbuckle	Kick (Repeating)
1	Head into Turnbuckle	Punch (Repeating)
1	Head into Turnbuckle	Tieup (Repeating)
5	Pump Handle Slam	Left, Tieup or Right, Tieup
5	Pump Handle Slam	Up, Tieup or Down, Tieup

From Corner (Running)

DAMAGE	NAME	MOVE
3	Charging Butt Bump	Kick
3	Charging Butt Bump	Punch
3	Charging Butt Bump	Tieup

Ready

DAMAGE	NAME	MOVE
6	Front Face DDT	Left, Right, Punch or Right, Left, Punch
3	Arm Drag	Up, Up, Punch
3	Crucifix	Left, Up, Tieup or Right, Up, Tieup
7	Double Underhook Suplex	Left, Right, Tieup or Right, Left, Tieup
5	Flying Head Scissors	Left, Up, Kick or Right, Up, Kick
3	Drop Toe Hold	Down, Down, Kick
6	Gut Wrench	Left, Up, Punch or Right, Up, Punch
4	Hiptoss	Up, Down, Tieup
2	Japanese Arm Drag	Down, Down, Punch
4	Knee to Face	Up, Down, Kick or Down, Up, Kick
4	Kneebreaker	Left, Down, Tieup or Right, Down, Tieup
3	Leg Drag	Left, Left, Kick or Right, Right, Kick
5	Neck Breaker	Up, Down, Tieup or Down, Up, Tieup
5	Reverse Pain Killer	Left, Down, Kick, or Right, Down, Kick
7	Vertical Suplex	Left, Left, Punch or Right, Right, Punch

Ground Holds (At Feet)

DAMAGE	NAME	MOVE
5	Elbow Drop Onto Leg	Left, Left, Kick or Right, Right, Kick
5	Elbow Drop Onto Leg	Up, Up, Kick or Down, Down, Kick
6	Leg Grapevine	Left, Right, Kick or Right, Left, Kick
6	Elbow to Groin	Up, Down, Kick or Down, Up, Kick
7	Wishbone Leg Splitter	Left, Up, Down, Kick or Right, Down, Up, Kick

Ground Holds (At Head)

DAMAGE	NAME	MOVE
5	Rear Chin Lock	Left, Left, Punch or Right, Right, Punch
5	Rear Chin Lock	Up, Up, Punch or Down, Down, Punch
6	Leg Lock Chokehold	Left, Right, Punch or Right, Left, Punch
6	Painkiller	Up, Down, Punch or Down, Up, Punch

Ground Hits (Standing)

DAMAGE	NAME	MOVE
3	Knee Drop	Down, Kick
1	Stomp	Kick
4	Standing Moonsault (at side)	Down, Punch
2	Elbow Drop	Punch

Ground Hits (Running)

DAMAGE	NAME	MOVE
3	Running Knee Drop	Kick
3	Fist Drop	Punch
4	Splash	Tieup

Running Opponent

DAMAGE	NAME	MOVE
5	Drop Kick Against Running	Kick
6	Back Body Drop	Punch
7	Power Slam	Tieup
8	Sidewalk Slam	Left, Punch, or Right, Punch

Kicks/Punches

DAMAGE	NAME	MOVE
3	Kick	Kick
5	Drop Kick	Up, Kick
3	Grab and Punch	Punch
5	Haymaker	Up, Punch or Down, Punch
2	Punch	Left, Punch or Right, Punch

Running

DAMAGE	NAME	MOVE
5	Spinning Neck Breaker	Kick
5	Running Clothesline	Punch
5	Tackle with Punches	Tieup

Turnbuckle (Opponent On Ground)

DAMAGE	NAME	MOVE
6	Kamikaze Headbutt	Kick
6	Kamikaze Headbutt	Punch
6	Kamikaze Headbutt	Tieup
7	Driving Elbow	Kick + Block

DAMAGE	NAME	MOVE
7	Splash	Punch + Tieup
8	Somersault Senton Splash	Up, Up, Punch + Kick

Turnbuckle (Opponent Standing)

DAMAGE	NAME	MOVE
6	Drop Kick Turnbuckle	Kick
6	Drop Kick Turnbuckle	Punch
6	Drop Kick Turnbuckle	Tieup
6	Drop Kick Turnbuckle	Kick + Block
7	Body Press (in front of opponent)	Kick + Block
7	Shoulder Tackle	Punch + Tieup
8	Hurricanranna	Left, Right, Kick + Tieup or Right, Left, Kick + Tieup
9	The Mosh Pit	Left, Right, Up, Tieup + Block
5	Moonsault	Block

Apron (Opponent On Ground)

DAMAGE	NAME	MOVE
6	Kamikaze Headbutt	Kick
6	Kamikaze Headbutt	Punch
6	Kamikaze Headbutt	Tieup
7	Driving Elbow	Kick + Block
7	Splash	Punch + Tieup

Apron (Opponent Standing)

DAMAGE	NAME	MOVE
6	Drop Kick Apron	Kick
6	Drop Kick Apron	Punch
6	Drop Kick Apron	Tieup
7	Body Press	Kick + Block
7	Shoulder Tackle	Punch + Tieup

Headbanger– Thrasher

The better half of the Headbanger headache, Thrasher is a bit speedier and has a tad more charisma (Hey, how can you not like someone who really knows  how to party?), but he lacks strength and toughness. His Brainbuster and Somersault Leg Drop are forces to be reckoned with, as are his Sidewalk Slam and Belly Back Suplex moves. However, those who can keep him from using his quickness to his advantage will win the match.

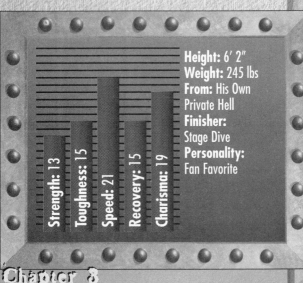

Height: 6' 2"
Weight: 245 lbs
From: His Own Private Hell
Finisher: Stage Dive
Personality: Fan Favorite

Strength: 13
Toughness: 15
Speed: 21
Recovery: 15
Charisma: 19

Behind Opponent

DAMAGE	NAME	MOVE
6	Russian Leg Sweep	Kick
6	Russian Leg Sweep	Punch
6	Russian Leg Sweep	Tieup
7	Neck Breaker	Left, Left, Kick or Right, Right, Kick
7	Neck Breaker	Up, Up, Kick or Down, Down, Kick
7	Reverse DDT	Left, Left, Punch or Right, Right, Punch
7	Reverse DDT	Up, Up, Punch or Down, Down, Punch
7	Side Slam	Left, Left, Tieup or Right, Right, Tieup
7	Side Slam	Up, Up, Tieup or Down, Down, Tieup
8	Belly Back Suplex	Left, Up, Right, Tieup or Right, Up, Left, Tieup

Tieup

DAMAGE	NAME	MOVE
1	Hiptoss	Kick
2	Neck Breaker	Punch
3	Inverted Atomic Drop	Tieup

DAMAGE	NAME	MOVE
4	Fisherman's Suplex	Left, Kick or Right, Kick
4	Fisherman's Suplex	Up, Kick or Down, Kick
5	Side Slam	Left, Punch or Right, Punch
5	Side Slam	Up, Punch or Down, Punch
6	Samoan Drop	Left, Tieup or Right, Tieup
6	Samoan Drop	Up, Tieup or Down, Tieup
7	Northern Lights Suplex	Left, Down, Kick or Right, Down, Kick
8	Sidewalk Slam	Left, Up, Punch or Right, Down, Punch
9	Brainbuster	Left, Up, Tieup or Right, Down, Tieup

Corner (Facing)

DAMAGE	NAME	MOVE
1	Chest Chop	Kick (Repeating)
1	Chest Chop	Punch (Repeating)
3	Splash In Corner	Tieup
5	Flying Head Scissors	Left, Left, Kick or Right, Right, Kick

DAMAGE	NAME	MOVE
5	Flying Head Scissors	Up, Up, Kick or Down, Down, Kick
5	Hurricanranna	Left, Left, Punch or Right, Right, Punch
5	Hurricanranna	Up, Up, Punch or Down, Down, Punch
5	Swinging DDT	Left, Left, Tieup or Right, Right, Tieup
5	Swinging DDT	Up, Up, Tieup or Down, Down, Tieup
7	Superplex	Left, Down, Right, Punch

Corner (Behind)

DAMAGE	NAME	MOVE
1	Head into Turnbuckle	Kick
1	Head into Turnbuckle	Punch
1	Head into Turnbuckle	Tieup
5	Pump Handle Slam	Left, Tieup or Right, Tieup
5	Pump Handle Slam	Up, Tieup or Down, Tieup

Corner (Running)

DAMAGE	NAME	MOVE
3	Charging Butt Bump	Kick
3	Charging Butt Bump	Punch
3	Charging Butt Bump	Tieup

DAMAGE	NAME	MOVE
6	Front Face DDT	Left, Right, Punch or Right, Left, Punch
2	Arm Wrench	Left, Up, Punch or Right, Up, Punch
3	Crucifix	Left, Up, Tieup or Right, Up, Tieup
3	Drop Toe Hold	Down, Down, Kick
4	Fireman's Carry	Left, Right, Kick or Right, Left, Kick
8	Hurricanranna	Left, Right, Up, Kick or Right, Left, Up, Kick
3	Headlock Takedown	Left, Down, Punch or Right, Down, Punch
2	Japanese Arm Drag	Down, Down, Punch
6	Overhead Belly Belly Suplex	Up, Down, Tieup or Down, Up, Tieup
5	Reverse Pain Killer	Left, Down, Kick or Right, Down, Kick
7	Sidewall Slam	Left, Down, Tieup or Right, Down, Tieup
6	Single Arm DDT	Left, Up, Kick or Right, Up, Kick
6	Spinebuster	Left, Right, Tieup or Right, Left, Tieup

Ground Holds
(At Feet)

DAMAGE	NAME	MOVE
5	Elbow to Groin	Left, Left, Kick or Right, Right, Kick
5	Elbow to Groin	Up, Up, Kick or Down, Down, Kick
6	Reverse Indian Deathlock	Left, Right, Kick or Right, Left, Kick
6	STF	Up, Down, Kick or Down, Up, Kick
7	Boston Crab	Left, Down, Right, Kick or Right, Down, Left, Kick

Ground Holds
(At Head)

DAMAGE	NAME	MOVE
5	Arm Wrench	Left, Left, Punch or Right, Right, Punch
5	Arm Wrench	Up, Up, Punch or Down, Down, Punch
6	Leg Lock Chokehold	Left, Right, Punch or Right, Left, Punch
6	Short Arm Scissor	Up, Down, Punch or Down, Up, Punch

Ground Hits
(Standing)

DAMAGE	NAME	MOVE
3	Leg Drop (at side)	Kick
1	Stomp	Kick
2	Fist Drop	Punch
4	Standing Moonsault (at side)	Down, Punch
3	Knee Drop	Down, Punch

Ground Hits
(Running)

DAMAGE	NAME	MOVE
4	Leg Drop (at side)	Kick
3	Running Knee Drop	Kick
3	Running Elbow Drop	Punch
3	Running Knee Drop	Tieup

Running Opponent

DAMAGE	NAME	MOVE
5	Drop Kick	Kick
5	Flying Back Elbow	Punch
7	Spinebuster	Tieup
8	Hurricanranna	Up, Kick or Down, Kick

Kicks/Punches

DAMAGE	NAME	MOVE
3	Kick	Kick
5	Drop Kick	Up, Kick
3	Grab and Punch	Punch
2	Inside Forearm	Left, Punch, or Right, Punch
5	Haymaker	Up, Punch or Down, Punch

Running

DAMAGE	NAME	MOVE
4	Flying Forearm	Kick
5	Flying Clothesline	Punch
5	Spinning Neck Breaker	Tieup

Turnbuckle (Opponent On Ground)

DAMAGE	NAME	MOVE
6	Elbow Drop	Kick
6	Elbow Drop	Punch
6	Elbow Drop	Tieup
7	Leg Drop	Kick + Block
7	Somersault Senton Splash	Punch + Tieup

DAMAGE	NAME	MOVE
8	Shooting Star Press	Up, Up, Kick + Tieup
9	Somersault Leg Drop	Left, Up, Up, Punch + Kick or Right, Up, Up, Punch + Kick

Turnbuckle (Opponent Standing)

DAMAGE	NAME	MOVE
6	Axhandle Smash	Kick
6	Axhandle Smash	Punch
6	Axhandle Smash	Tieup
7	Body Press (in front of opponent)	Kick + Block
7	Torpedo Drop Kick	Kick + Block
3	Sunset Flip (in front of opponent)	Punch + Tieup
7	Torpedo Drop Kick	Punch + Tieup
8	Hurricanranna	Left, Up, Kick + Tieup or Right, Up, Kick + Tieup

Apron (Opponent On Ground)

DAMAGE	NAME	MOVE
6	Elbow Drop	Kick
6	Elbow Drop	Punch
6	Elbow Drop	Tieup
7	Leg Drop	Kick + Block
7	Somersault Senton Splash	Punch + Tieup

Apron (Opponent Standing)

DAMAGE	NAME	MOVE
6	Axhandle Smash	Kick
6	Axhandle Smash	Punch
6	Axhandle Smash	Tieup
7	Body Press (in front of opponent)	Kick + Block
6	Axhandle Smash	Kick + Block
7	Torpedo Drop Kick	Punch + Tieup

Kàne

Although he hides his disfigured face behind a mask, there's no mistaking that Kane is The Undertaker's brother. Not only does he have almost identical stats,

whether it's his height or his strength, in WWF War Zone, he also has the same exact move list as his Fan Favorite flesh-and-blood.

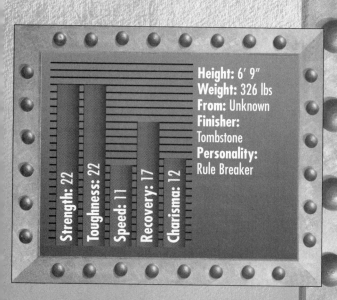

Height: 6′ 9″
Weight: 326 lbs
From: Unknown
Finisher: Tombstone
Personality: Rule Breaker

Strength: 22
Toughness: 22
Speed: 11
Recovery: 17
Charisma: 12

Behind Opponent

DAMAGE	NAME	MOVE
6	Neck Breaker	Kick
6	Neck Breaker	Punch
6	Neck Breaker	Tieup
7	Reverse DDT	Left, Left, Kick or Right, Right, Kick
7	Reverse DDT	Up, Up, Kick or Down, Down, Kick
7	Reverse DDT	Left, Left, Punch or Right, Right, Punch
7	Reverse DDT	Up, Up, Punch or Down, Down, Punch
8	Side Slam	Left, Left, Up, Tieup or Right, Right, Up, Tieup

Tieup

DAMAGE	NAME	MOVE
1	Back Breaker	Kick
2	Atomic Drop	Punch
3	Sidewalk Slam	Tieup
4	Northern Lights Suplex	Left, Kick or Right Kick
4	Northern Lights Suplex	Up, Kick or Down, Kick
5	DDT	Left, Punch or Right, Punch
5	DDT	Up, Punch or Down, Punch

Kane

161

DAMAGE	NAME	MOVE
6	Gut Wrench Power Bomb	Left, Tieup or Right, Tieup
6	Gut Wrench Power Bomb	Up, Tieup or Down, Tieup
7	Vertical Suplex	Left, Down, Kick or Right, Down, Kick
8	Overhead Belly Belly Suplex	Left, Up, Punch or Right, Up, Punch
9	Choke Slam	Left, Right, Tieup or Right, Left, Tieup
9	Tombstone Piledriver	Up, Down, Tieup or Down, Up, Tieup

Corner (Facing)

DAMAGE	NAME	MOVE
3	Choke with Boot	Kick
1	Climb and Pummel	Punch (Repeating)
3	Choke with Boot	Tieup
5	Overhead Press	Left, Left, Kick or Right, Right, Kick
5	Overhead Press	Up, Up, Kick or Down, Down, Kick
5	Belly Belly Suplex	Left, Left, Punch or Right, Right, Punch

DAMAGE	NAME	MOVE
5	Belly Belly Suplex	Up, Up, Punch or Down, Down, Punch
5	Top Rope Double Underhook	Left, Left, Tieup or Right, Right, Tieup
5	Top Rope Double Underhook	Up, Up, Tieup or Down, Down, Tieup
7	Top Rope Superplex	Up, Up, Down, Kick or Down, Down, Up, Kick

Corner (Behind)

DAMAGE	NAME	MOVE
1	Head into Turnbuckle	Kick (Repeating)
1	Head into Turnbuckle	Punch (Repeating)
1	Head into Turnbuckle	Tieup (Repeating)
5	Pump Handle Slam	Left, Tieup or Right, Tieup
5	Pump Handle Slam	Up, Tieup or Down, Tieup

Corner (Running)

DAMAGE	NAME	MOVE
3	Charging Clothesline	Kick
3	Charging Clothesline	Punch
3	Charging Clothesline	Tieup

Ready

DAMAGE	NAME	MOVE
6	Front Face DDT	Left, Left, Tieup or Right, Right, Tieup
6	Overhead Belly Belly Suplex	Left, Down, Tieup or Right, Down, Tieup
6	Choke Slam	Down, Down, Punch
7	DDT	Left, Down, Kick or Right, Down, Kick
6	Gut Wrench	Left, Right, Punch or Right, Left, Punch
5	Neck Breaker	Left, Down, Punch or Right, Down, Punch
6	Side Belly Belly Suplex	Left, Right, Tieup or Right, Left, Tieup
5	Short Arm Clothesline	Left, Up, Tieup or Right, Up, Tieup
6	Single Arm DDT	Left, Up, Kick or Right, Up, Kick
5	Snap Mare	Left, Up, Punch or Right, Up, Punch
6	Throat Toss	Down, Up, Tieup
9	Tombstone Piledriver	Down, Down, Down, Punch + Tieup
7	Vertical Suplex	Left, Right, Kick or Right, Left, Kick

Ground Holds (At Feet)

DAMAGE	NAME	MOVE
5	Elbow Drop Onto Leg	Left, Left, Kick or Right, Right, Kick
5	Elbow Drop Onto Leg	Up, Up, Kick or Down, Down, Kick
6	Half Crab	Left, Right, Kick or Right, Left, Kick
6	Surfboard	Up, Down, Kick or Down, Up, Kick
7	Leg Lock	Left, Right, Left, Kick or Right, Left, Right, Kick

Ground Holds (At Head)

DAMAGE	NAME	MOVE
5	Arm Wrench	Left, Left, Punch or Right, Right, Punch
5	Arm Wrench	Up, Up, Punch or Down, Down, Punch
6	Squeeze Head	Left, Right, Punch or Right, Left, Punch
6	Painkiller	Up, Down, Punch or Down, Up, Punch

Kane

165

Ground Hits (Standing)

DAMAGE	NAME	MOVE
3	Leg Drop (at side)	Kick
1	Stomp	Kick
3	Knee Drop	Down, Kick
2	Elbow Drop	Punch

Ground Hits (Running)

DAMAGE	NAME	MOVE
4	Leg Drop (at side)	Kick
3	Fist Drop	Kick
3	Fist Drop	Punch
4	Falling Headbutt	Tieup

Running Opponent

DAMAGE	NAME	MOVE
4	Boot to Face	Kick
5	Clothesline	Punch
7	Powerslam	Tieup
8	Spinebuster	Left, Tieup or Right, Tieup

Kicks/Punches

DAMAGE	NAME	MOVE
2	Quick Kick	Kick
3	Kick	Left, Kick or Right Kick
6	Thrust to Throat	Punch
3	Choke	Up, Punch or Down, Punch
5	Haymaker	Left, Punch, or Right, Punch

Running

DAMAGE	NAME	MOVE
5	Flying Clothesline	Punch
5	Flying Clothesline	Kick
5	Spinning Neck Breaker	Tieup

Turnbuckle (Opponent On Ground)

DAMAGE	NAME	MOVE
6	Fist Drop	Kick
6	Fist Drop	Punch
6	Fist Drop	Tieup

Kane

DAMAGE	NAME	MOVE
7	Double Foot Stomp	Kick + Block
7	Splash	Punch + Tieup
8	Driving Elbow	Left, Right, Kick + Tieup or Right, Left, Kick + Tieup

Turnbuckle (Opponent Standing)

DAMAGE	NAME	MOVE
6	Drop Kick Turnbuckle	Kick
6	Drop Kick Turnbuckle	Punch
6	Drop Kick Turnbuckle	Tieup
7	Axhandle Smash	Kick + Block
7	Clothesline Turnbuckle	Punch + Tieup
8	Forearm Smash	Left, Right, Kick + Tieup or Right, Left, Kick + Tieup

Apron (Opponent On Ground)

DAMAGE	NAME	MOVE
6	Fist Drop	Kick
6	Fist Drop	Punch
6	Fist Drop	Tieup

DAMAGE	NAME	MOVE
7	Double Foot Stomp	Kick + Block
7	Splash	Punch + Tieup

Apron (Opponent Standing)

DAMAGE	NAME	MOVE
6	Drop Kick Apron	Kick
6	Drop Kick Apron	Punch
6	Drop Kick Apron	Tieup
7	Axhandle Smash	Kick + Block
7	Clothesline Apron	Punch + Tieup

Kane

Ahmed Johnson

He may only be 6' 2" but don't think that all 300 plus pounds is all fat and flab. Ahmed is strong and tough, plus he knows a thing or two about winning wrestling matches. However, little is known about

Ahmed and he prefers to keep it that way. Be warned that he has more than his fair share of killer moves.

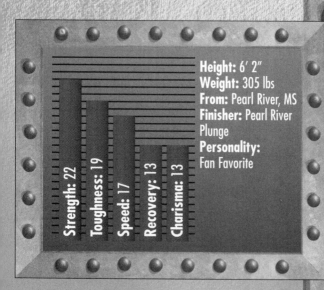

Height: 6' 2"
Weight: 305 lbs
From: Pearl River, MS
Finisher: Pearl River Plunge
Personality: Fan Favorite

Strength: 22
Toughness: 19
Speed: 17
Recovery: 13
Charisma: 13

Behind Opponent

DAMAGE	NAME	MOVE
6	Neck Breaker	Kick
6	Neck Breaker	Punch
6	Neck Breaker	Tieup
7	Pump Handle Slam	Left, Left, Kick or Right, Right, Kick
7	Pump Handle Slam	Up, Up, Kick or Down, Down, Kick
7	Reverse DDT	Left, Left, Punch or Right, Right, Punch
7	Reverse DDT	Up, Up, Punch or Down, Down, Punch
3	Victory Roll	Left, Left, Tieup or Right, Right, Tieup
3	Victory Roll	Up, Up, Tieup or Down, Down, Tieup
8	German Suplex	Left, Left, Up, Tieup or Right, Right, Up, Tieup

Tieup

DAMAGE	NAME	MOVE
1	Hiptoss	Kick
2	Neck Breaker	Punch
3	Gut Wrench Power Bomb	Tieup
4	Sidewalk Slam	Left, Kick or Right Kick

DAMAGE	NAME	MOVE
4	Sidewalk Slam	Up, Kick or Down, Kick
5	Samoan Drop	Left, Punch or Right, Punch
5	Samoan Drop	Up, Punch or Down, Punch
6	Vertical Suplex	Left, Tieup or Right, Tieup
6	Vertical Suplex	Up, Tieup or Down, Tieup
7	Brainbuster	Left, Up, Kick or Right, Up, Kick
8	Double Underhook Suplex	Left, Right, Punch or Right, Left, Punch
9	Power Bomb	Left, Down, Tieup or Right, Down, Tieup

Corner (Facing)

DAMAGE	NAME	MOVE
1	Chest Chop	Kick (Repeating)
1	Chest Chop	Punch (Repeating)
3	Splash In Corner	Tieup
5	Monkey Flip	Left, Left, Kick or Right, Right, Kick
5	Monkey Flip	Up, Up, Kick or Down, Down, Kick

DAMAGE	NAME	MOVE
5	Belly Belly Suplex	Left, Left, Punch or Right, Right, Punch
5	Belly Belly Suplex	Up, Up, Punch or Down, Down, Punch
5	Top Rope Superplex	Left, Left, Tieup or Right, Right, Tieup
5	Top Rope Superplex	Up, Up, Tieup or Down, Down, Tieup
7	Hurricanranna	Left, Right, Down, Kick or Right, Left, Down, Kick

Corner (Behind)

DAMAGE	NAME	MOVE
1	Head into Turnbuckle	Kick (Repeating)
1	Head into Turnbuckle	Punch (Repeating)
1	Head into Turnbuckle	Tieup (Repeating)
5	Pump Handle Slam	Left, Tieup or Right, Tieup
5	Pump Handle Slam	Up, Tieup or Down, Tieup

Corner (Running)

DAMAGE	NAME	MOVE
3	Charging Butt Bump	Kick
3	Charging Butt Bump	Punch
3	Charging Butt Bump	Tieup

Ahmed Johnson

173

DAMAGE	NAME	MOVE
6	Front Face DDT	Left, Right, Punch or Right, Left, Punch
3	Arm Drag	Up, Up, Punch
3	Crucifix	Left, Up, Tieup or Right, Up, Tieup
7	Double Underhook Suplex	Left, Right, Tieup or Right, Left, Tieup
5	Flying Head Scissors	Left, Up, Kick or Right, Up, Kick
3	Drop Toe Hold	Down, Down, Kick
6	Gut Wrench	Left, Up, Punch or Right, Up, Punch
4	Hiptoss	Up, Down, Tieup
2	Japanese Arm Drag	Down, Down, Punch
4	Knee to Face	Up, Down, Kick or Down, Up, Kick
4	Kneebreaker	Left, Down, Tieup or Right, Down, Tieup
3	Leg Drag	Left, Left, Kick or Right, Right, Kick
5	Neck Breaker	Up, Up, Tieup or Down, Down, Tieup
5	Reverse Pain Killer	Left, Down, Kick or Right, Down, Kick
7	Vertical Suplex	Left, Left, Punch or Right, Right, Punch

Ground Holds (At Feet)

DAMAGE	NAME	MOVE
5	Elbow Drop Onto Leg	Left, Left, Kick or Right, Right, Kick
5	Elbow Drop Onto Leg	Up, Up, Kick or Down, Down, Kick
6	Leg Grapevine	Left, Right, Kick or Right, Left, Kick
6	Elbow to Groin	Up, Down, Kick or Down, Up, Kick
7	Wishbone Leg Splitter	Left, Up, Down, Kick or Right, Down, Up, Kick

Ground Holds (At Head)

DAMAGE	NAME	MOVE
5	Rear Chin Lock	Left, Left, Punch or Right, Right, Punch
5	Rear Chin Lock	Up, Up, Punch or Down, Down, Punch
6	Leg Lock Chokehold	Left, Right, Punch or Right, Left, Punch
6	Painkiller	Up, Down, Punch or Down, Up, Punch

Ground Hits (Standing)

DAMAGE	NAME	MOVE
3	Knee Drop	Down, Kick
1	Stomp	Kick

Apron (Opponent On Ground)

DAMAGE	NAME	MOVE
6	Kamikaze Headbutt	Kick
6	Kamikaze Headbutt	Punch
6	Kamikaze Headbutt	Tieup
7	Driving Elbow	Kick + Block
7	Splash	Punch + Tieup

Apron (Opponent Standing)

DAMAGE	NAME	MOVE
6	Drop Kick Apron	Kick
6	Drop Kick Apron	Punch
6	Drop Kick Apron	Tieup
7	Body Press	Kick + Block
7	Shoulder Tackle	Punch + Tieup